exodyssey

VISUAL DEVELOPMENT OF AN EPIC ADVENTURE BY **STEAMBOT STUDIOS**

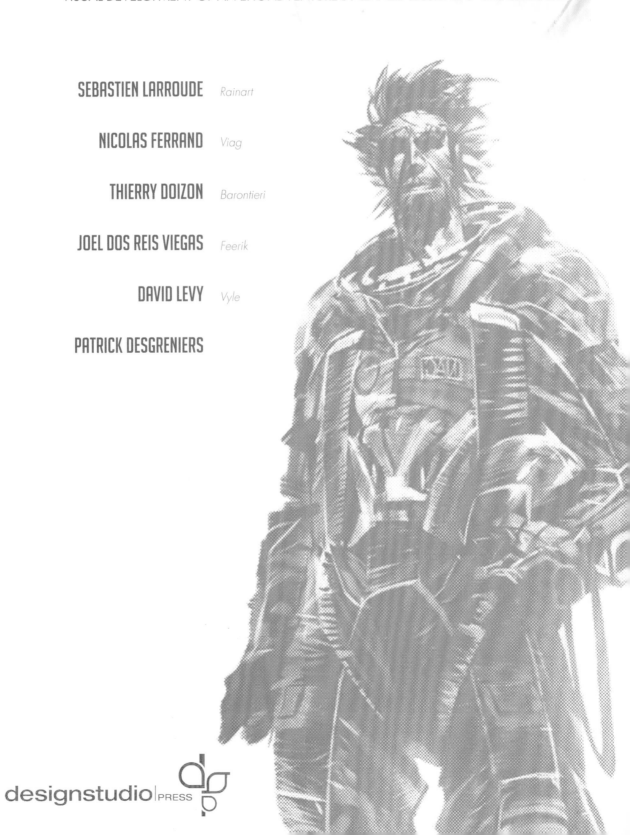

SEBASTIEN LARROUDE *Rainart*

NICOLAS FERRAND *Viag*

THIERRY DOIZON *Barontieri*

JOEL DOS REIS VIEGAS *Feerik*

DAVID LEVY *Vyle*

PATRICK DESGRENIERS

designstudio PRESS

DEDICATION

"To our families and girlfriends who have supported us since the beginning, you have made this book possible."

exodyssey
visual develpoment of an epic adventure by
Steambot Studios

Graphic Design: Joel Dos Reis Viegas
Copy Editing: Kate Soto
Editor: Scott Robertson

Published by
Design Studio Press
8577 Higuera Street
Culver City, CA 90232

Website: www.designstudiopress.com
E-mail: info@designstudiopress.com

Printed in China: First edition, April 2009

10 9 8 7 6 5 4 3 2

soft cover ISBN 978-1-933492-39-1
hard cover ISBN 978-1-933492-40-7

Library of Congress Control Number: 2008943963

TABLE OF CONTENTS

FOREWORD

Self-motivation, teamwork, design, drawing and rendering skills of the highest caliber: this is what comes to mind when I think of the members of Steambot Studios.

It is a proud moment in my young publishing company's history to be able to bring you such a fabulous body of work as presented within the covers of Exodyssey. Aside from the beautiful renderings and the cutting-edge designs, what makes this book special is that it was executed by a group of concept designers entirely on their own personal time, without pay, and most important to our benefit...they pulled it off!

In recent years I have had some personal experience pooling talent toward a common goal, and it is no simple task. Looking at this finished book, I feel it holds up well against any of the numerous "art of" movie books now in print. In many ways it excels beyond these books due to the main strengths of this studio: teamwork, originality and experimentation of the creative process.

By their free-flowing exchange of ideas and techniques, the Steambot team inspires each other in their unending pursuit of creative image making. No tools or methods are considered the "end-all" for them, instead they strive to invent, re-imagine, mix, mash and compel each other, and now us, with new and unique ways to create our own fantasy worlds. Whether it is building custom brushes in Photoshop or abstract 3-D forms in the digital world, I am grateful to learn about the processes they have explored, as I know many of my students will be as well.

My hope for this book is that it will inspire not only individuals to share their ideas and processes with the rest of us through the Internet but that it will lead to the formation of more of these small studios who have whole-heartedly undertaken the pursuit of design and artistic excellence in the area of entertainment design. Once only the domain of large movie studios with ridiculous budgets, I think this book demonstrates a fire and passion for the subject rarely seen before, which they executed with such brilliant teamwork and creativity. I congratulate the members of Steambot for completing this very personal project which represents many lost weekends and financial sacrifice. You have done a great thing; thank you for sharing.

November 2008, Los Angeles

Scott Robertson
Founder, Design Studio Press
Chair of Entertainment Design, Art Center College of Design

Exodyssey is the name given to the long and war-filled period of time during which humans departed for exo-planets in order to survive their own destruction. The Earth had long been pushed to the edge of extinction by political conflict, pollution and nuclear waste infecting even the most remote areas: the only way to survive was to flee and start anew.

This book chronicles the journey of Harry, a highly gifted engineer with a violent past as a *Nudrift* racer. He is a descendant of the first wave of colonists who decided to leave Earth, having foreseen the demise of humanity. The mysterious circumstances surrounding the disappearance of their spacecraft, which housed hundreds of families in reduced temporal sleep and had enough technology to reconstruct a new humanity, became a closely-guarded state secret known only to a select few outside the inner circle of power of the self-proclaimed emperor, Menauphis.

A hundred years have passed on a terminally sick Earth, and those other descendants such as Harry have all been "removed" by the newly proclaimed emperor, Menauphis' son. The question is, "Why?" Only Harry remains as the sole-surviving descendant of those ill-fated colonists. Lately he has been receiving messages in the form of nightmares first, then by visiting apparitions, and finally by coded radio communications. During the hunt for Harry his wife disappears, probably killed by the Earth police who actively work for the emperor. In addition to hunting Harry, the Earth Police have been trying to remove any possible humanitarian ideology that might survive by destroying any cultural media disapproved by the emperor, a.k.a. the S.O.L. ruling body.

Lately the visiting apparitions are affecting not only our hero, but the entire solar system. They resonate like anything but friendly messages: death images, horrible creatures and dark warfare machines; the whole solar system is on the brink of total panic and collapse, the dictatorship can barely keep hold of the population. Harry's wife sometimes appears to him through his nightmares, urging him to find her. Partly thinking he has gone mad, and partly following his heart, he decides to join the mass exodus and fight his way through the mayhem of a dying humanity in order to confront the emperor, find answers to his lost origins and return to his loved one. Through this odyssey, he will discover such friends as CET (a mining robot), will race Nudrifts and build a dysfunctional team of followers.

As the army learns that Harry is the key to discovering the origins of an extra-terrestrial invasion, they decide to keep him alive and give him the means to travel to the planet code-named "Samhuinn." Under the very close scrutiny of Puhell, one of the emperor's secret advisors, our group of dysfunctional heroes will, unknowingly, serve in the army's command to search and destroy the potential threat the aliens represent to the emperor.

ENGLISH

We'd like to start by thanking you for your ongoing loyalty and your ever-increasing interest in the Steambot adventure and its founding members. Steambot is the result of a vision that is now alive and kicking, and this book is here to tell you our story.

Steambot is a combination of six artists coming from diverse artistic backgrounds, who have been working for more than a decade in the video game, film, and animated-movie industries (E.A., NC soft, Ubisoft, Overbook, Reel FX, Edge of Reality, Cryptids, Disney Channel, Walt Disney Imagineering, Kings Isle Studios, Canal+, Blue Sky, Hasbro, abc family, Activision, etc.). The team's success stems from our career choices, which have helped us innovate and push the limits of concept art and design. The know-how required to use 3-D tools to animate, compose, and structure ideas is of indisputable value. This knowledge has allowed Steambot to rise prominently within the industry. The desire to share, teach, and learn is a key incentive when we work, and we are proud to have helped a number of young artists through our DVD (Gnomom) and our live demos at conferences and seminars over the last couple of years (e.g., Adapt, Siggraph, Gnomom Workshop, University of Applied Arts of Vienna).

This book is more than just concept art to us. It reflects our achievements in terms of teamwork, quest for identity, and artistic growth. It has been part of our lives for the past three years, along with our daytime jobs, our trips, our girlfriends, family, and friends.

We bring you a unique and vibrant vision of a world that we hope will appeal to your imagination. We hope you'll enjoy discovering it as much as we have enjoyed creating it.

A thousand thanks, and make sure your seatbelt is properly fastened. ...

The Steambot Team

FRENCH

Tout d'abord nous tenons particulièrement à vous remercier de votre fidélité et de votre intérêt grandissant à l'égard de Steambot et de tous ses fondateurs. Steambot existe, fruit d'une réelle vision, et cet ouvrage est là pour en temoigner.

Steambot c'est six artistes venus de divers horizons artistiques, oeuvrant depuis plus de 10 ans dans l'industrie du jeu video, du cinéma et du film d'animation (E.A, NC soft, Ubisoft, Overbook, Reel FX, Edge Of Reality, Cryptids, Disney Channel, Walt Disney Imagineering, Kings Isle Studios, Canal+, Blue Sky, Hasbro, abc family, Activision, etc ...). Le parcours de chacun apporte énormément au sein de l'équipe, et permet d'innover et de pousser sans cesse les limites artistiques et techniques du concept art. Savoir utiliser la 3-D à bon escient, animer, compositer, structurer nos idées sont des richesses indiscutables qui permettent aujourd'hui à Steambot de pouvoir s'imposer dans l'industrie. L'envie de partager, d'enseigner et d'apprendre est un atout majeur pour nous, et nous sommes fiers d'avoir permis à nombre de jeunes artistes d'évoluer grâce à nos DVD (gnomom) et à nos démonstrations live durant les conférences et séminaires ces dernières années (Adapt, Siggraph, Gnomon workshop, University of Applied Arts of Vienna...).

Plus qu'un livre de concept art, cet ouvrage représente l'aboutissement d'un travail d'équipe, d'une recherche d'identité et la maturité artistique de chacun. Il représente aussi trois années de recherche partagées entre emplois, voyages, familles, amis et conjoints.

Nous vous livrons ici une vision unique et pertinente d'un monde qui, nous l'espérons, saura vous séduire et éveiller votre curiosité, et que vous prendrez autant de plaisir à découvrir que celui que nous avons eu à le créer.

Merci mille fois, et attachez bien vôtre ceinture...

L'equipage Steambot

SPANISH

Nos gustaría comenzar por agradecer a todas las personas que han mostrado un interés constante en la aventura de Steambot y que han apoyado a sus creadores. Steambot es el resultado de una visión que hoy en día es una realidad, y la intención de este libro es contar su historia.

Steambot es la combinación de seis artistas emergentes de diversos campos que han trabajado por mas de una década en la industria de los juegos de video, cine y animación cinematográfica (E.A, NC soft, Ubisoft, Overbook, Reel FX, Edge Of Reality, Cryptids, Disney Channel, Walt Disney Imagineering, Kings Isle Studios, Canal+, Blue Sky, Hasbro, abc family, Activision, etc …). El éxito del equipo radica en nuestras competencias profesionales que nos ha ayudado a ir mas allá en términos conceptuales, incluyendo la capacidad para utilizar la 3-D y para hacer animación, y es por esto que Steambot tiene la capacidad de ocupar un lugar destacado en la industria. Dentro de las principales motivaciones en nuestro trabajo esta el deseo de compartir, enseñar y aprender, y nos sentimos orgullosos de haber ayudado a varios jóvenes artistas a través de nuestro DVD "Gnomon", y de nuestras demostraciones en vivo que hemos tenido la oportunidad de realizar en el transcurso de los últimos años (Adapt, Siggraph, Gnomom Workshop, Univeristy of Applied Arts of Vienna…).

Este libro es para nosotros mas que una muestra de nuestro trabajo conceptual, en el se reflejan nuestros logros como equipo, nuestra búsqueda de identidad y nuestro desarrollo artístico. Este libro ha sido parte de nuestras vidas por los últimos tres anos; de la misma manera que lo han sido nuestros trabajos, viajes, compañeros, familia y amigos. Queremos presentar una imagen del mundo vibrante y única con la que esperamos que los lectores se identifiquen e igualmente esperamos que disfruten descubriendo las ideas de la misma manera como hemos disfrutado creándolas.

Muchas gracias y esperamos que tengan el cinturón de seguridad debidamente ajustado…

El equipo de Steambot

JAPANESE

まず初めにSteambotの活動そしてメンバーに注目してくれた皆さん、大変ありがとうございます。Steambot
はメンバーのビジョンを元に日々変化して行きます。この本はその日々の変化を記録した物です。

Steambot
とは六人のメンバーから成り立っています。メンバーはそれぞれ違う所でスキルを磨いてきましたが全員ゲーム、映画業界で10年以上の経験を持つ者ばかりです。(E.A, NC soft, Ubisoft, Overbook, Reel FX, Edge Of Reality, Cryptids, Disney Channel, Walt Disney Imagineering, Kings Isle Studios, Canal+, Blue Sky, Hasbro, abc family, Activision等)
このチームの成功の裏には業界で培ったノウハウがあります。3D、アニメーション、アイディアの確立そして表現する能力等コンセプトアートのイノベーションそして限界に挑戦するのに全て無くてはならないものでした。このノウハウがあるからこそSteambotはここまで来れた物だと我々は理解しています。だからこそSteambotはアーティストの育成に協力したいと考えています。今までにも教材用ＤＶＤ(Gnomon)、ライブデモ、セミナーなど通して若いアーティスト達と関わることが出来ました。(Adapt, Siggraph, Gnomon Workshop, Univeristy of Applied Arts of Vienna等)

この本は我々にとってはただ単に作品を集めただけの本ではありません。今までチームとして活動してきた軌跡でありチームワーク、アイデンティティー探し、そしてアーティストとしての成長の証でもあります。
過去三年間この本は仕事、彼女、家族と共に我々の生活の一部でした。我々はユニークで活き活きとした世界観を皆さんにお届けします。メンバーそれぞれ楽しんで作った物なので皆さんのイマジネーションに訴えかけ楽しんで見て頂ければ大変うれしいです。

この本を手にとってくれて本当にありがとうございます、ここからは揺れますのでシートベルトをしっかりお締めください。

Steambot

Earth　　Moon　　Mars　　Black Hole Station　　Samhuinn　　Spa...

End

Introduction　　Preparation and Conflict　　Discovery　　Finale

The timetable shows a simplified version of our storyline. Harry's epic journey starts in the S.O.L. Empire and is divided into five main chapters. Now welcome aboard, fasten your seat belts, and enjoy the adventure!

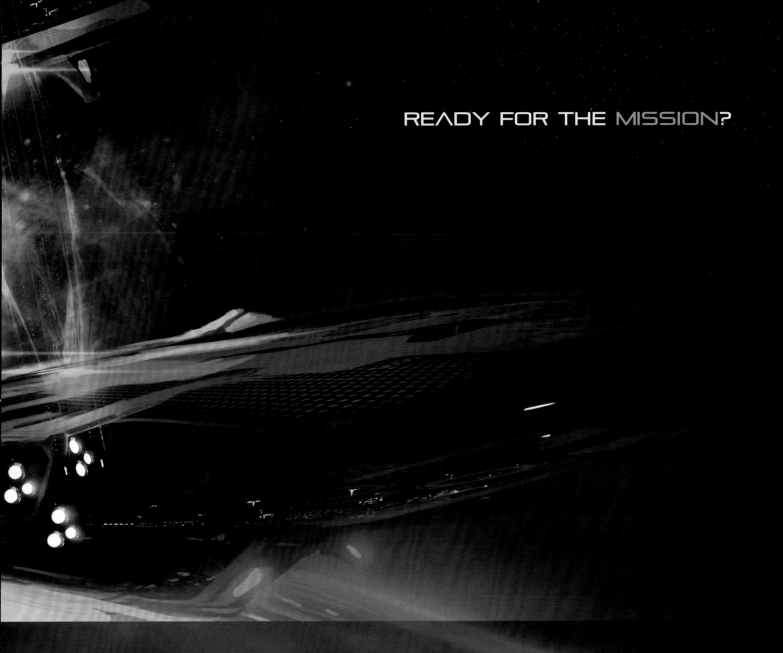

THE STORY

▷ The mission assigned to our heroes (a dysfunctional team of prisoners, pilots, and scientists) is to discover the truth lying behind the appearances, political problems, power, and technology of the Empire. The apparent peace created by the Solar System Organization (originally from Earth and now on Mars) hides the heroes' real plans, and is shaken by the discovery of a new race that seems to spy on humans while adorning strange costumes that are entirely inspired by Halloween. As can be expected, those extra-terrestrial apparitions make humans panic. They assume the apparitions are a bad omen and organize their army to protect themselves and/or destroy those "monsters." One issue: the monster's planet, Sahmuinn, is light years away, and no current technology will allow them to travel that far. Humans will need a new travel system, and will eventually discover what lies on that mysterious planet—inhabitants who are probably more human than they are.

ESCAPE FROM EARTH

We are 200. We departed around 7:15 this morning, leaving everything behind us, bringing only our wives and children.
The journey is a nightmare. I can't believe this ship can reach the Moon. We don't know what to expect when arriving in
Neil Armstrong City (N.A.C.). This whole trip makes no sense now but I need to believe.

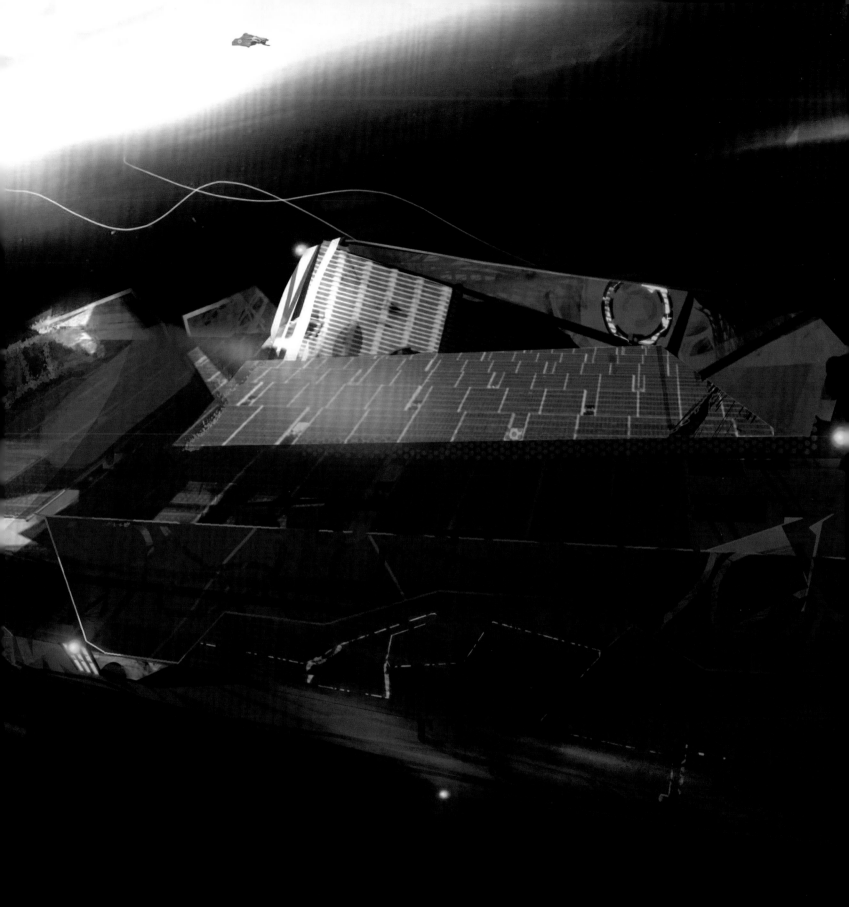

CHAPTER ONE

THE LANDSCAPES

Mood 1, 2, and 3: Gray values, desaturated. Green/yellow pollution layer and final comp, bright ochre by **Rainart.** Mood 4: **Rainart's** disaffected area speedpainting

Power plant structure (above) and pencil/marker sketches (below) by **Barontieri**

Paintover by **Barontieri** over the top of an industrial complex made by **Rainart**

Above: Heavily guarded S.O.L. electric power station by **Barontieri**
Right: Hyper-structure Space harbor at sunset, mood painting by **Rainart**

Rainart: *"Green City is a very old picture. I made this piece at the same time as the ARCHEON, between 2004 and 2005. It represents an abandoned city.* **Barontieri** *did a paintover with a structure on the top, and the cables hanging from the walls enabled mercenaries hiding in the buildings to escape easily. The concept of the structure is that of a huge web landed atop a forest's canopy. In the end, I created a short cinematic effect with a camera mapping technique and some composing tests we presented at the ADAPT 2006 conference in Montreal."*

Top left, **Vyle:** *"In a parallel to Portuguese ships leaving for a better world, the ships here have been replaced by mechanical docks and boat-like space vessels. The timeless subject of humanity in motion here reaches a cartoon-like dimension."*

Top right, **Vyle:** *"Driven by despair or hope, passengers regularly line up and eagerly await a ship that most probably will never reach its destination. Representing the play of order and chaos through light and shape has become a **Steambot** trademark. By playing with the exposure and scale elements (characters), a mood suddenly takes shape."*

HARRY'S LAIR

Above: External view of the loft by **Feerik**
Right page: Storyboard by **Feerik**

3-D Scene and color set: **Viag** and **Vyle**

"Sometimes I wake up and think about her...why? Why so early?"

"What was his goal, he who took your life away from me?...Please tell me, Claire."

"These dreams, always the same dreams...I have to do something!"

THE INTERIOR

This huge loft really defines Harry's personality, a loner who is passionate about mechanics and technology. We wanted the feel of an old, dusty and messy place filled with tons of mechanical objects and souvenirs of Harry's former life as a Nudrift champion. **Viag** gave us a fully rendered 3-D scene (global illumination), then **Feerik** and **Rainart** added a lot of new elements and believable details in their paintovers.

Paintover on 3-D by **Feerik**

Based on **Viag's** 3-D scene, **Cédric** and **Stéphanie Seaut** (two great 3-D artists) helped us to add a lot of elements and polish the final look of the loft.

Paintover on 3-D by **Rainart**

The kitchen area. All of the loft space was modeled by **Cédric** and **Stéphanie Séaut.**

Harry's desk and computers, concept by **Vyle**

Feerik: *"Keeping the original direction, my vision of Harry moved toward something more stylized. Finally, I have no preference between both characters. For the black-and-white sketches, I wanted an old-fashioned but charismatic feel for it, so I checked references from the past. I have a fascination for classic heroes (C. Heston in Ben-Hur or Planet of the Apes, or Clint Eastwood in general). I kept working in this direction for the colored versions, too, and I'm pretty sure it could look better on screen with these simpler and edgier shapes."*

Vyle: *"Entirely inspired by **Feerik**, this vision of Harry was meant to represent his deep personality and honest will. It follows the template of astronauts in my favorite movie, The Right Stuff."*

HARRY VICARE

Our hero is a 30-year-old enigmatic pilot whose nationality and origins are uncertain. He has an athletic build, unkempt hair, and dark-red cybernetic eyes. He has a dry sense of humor and often appears grumpy and clumsy. This, however, is mainly a disguise, as he is actually a natural leader with a penchant for military strategy and combat tactics. A few years back, Harry worked as a mercenary for the Republic of Asia but has since escaped Earth illegally aboard the Exodus.

This page: Concept by **Feerik**
Left page: Design variations by **Barontieri** (top), close up by **Vyle** (color), black and white sketches by **Feerik**

HARRY BY DAVID GIRAUD

SB team: *"When we decided to give to David Giraud (aka Mojette for those who know him on the forums) the responsibility of sculpting Harry, we already knew that the final result was going to meet our expectations. All of us had the chance to work with him at Ubisoft Montreal on various games, such as Assassin's Creed, Splinter Cell, and Prince of Persia. David is one of those 3-D artists as good in 2-D as in 3-D. He was a concept artist before becoming an accomplished 3-D artist/sculptor."*

Harry sculpted and posed in Pixologic ZBrush®

Left side   Back   Right side

Above: Model sheet of Harry (using **Feerik's** design as reference) by **Barontieri**
Below: 3-D model sculpted, textured, and rendered in Zbrush 3.1® by **David Giraud**

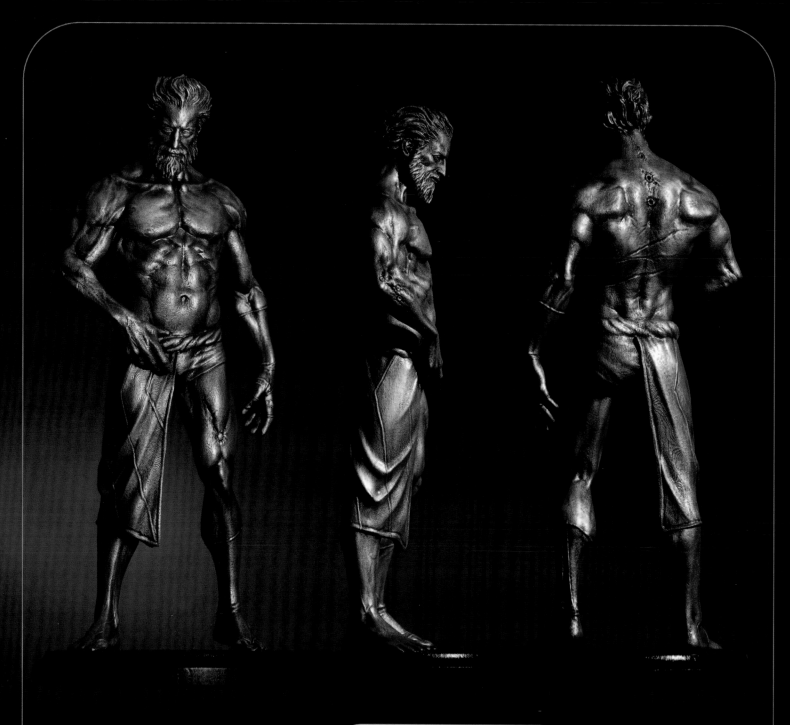

Photographer: **Duncan Turner**

FROM 3-D...TO REALITY

SB team: *"To get a real sculpture of Harry is something that means a lot to us. We are all fans of toys and collectibles. It was possible thanks to* **Offload Studios** *(www.offloadstudios.com). David Giraud was in contact with them. They really enjoyed the character, and they decided to make a 3-D print for the Siggraph conference, where David did a live demo as well. To have the sculpture in your hands gives another dimension to your work. It finally exists."*

Photographer: **Duncan Turner**

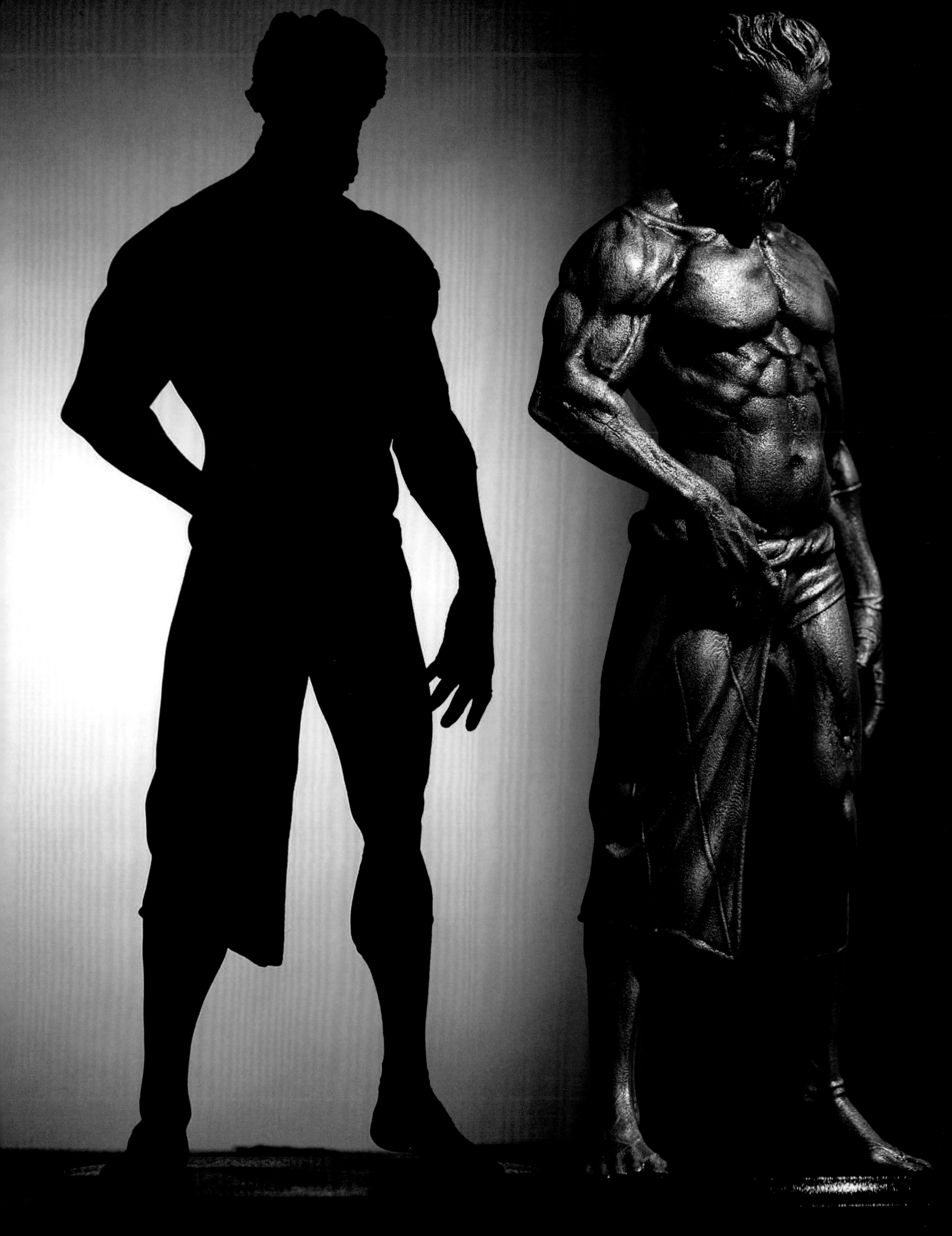

S.O.L. PILOTS

Barontieri: In this era of flying spacecrafts, being a pilot has become very trendy again. This has led to sharing increasingly limited sky access, which has generated a lot of competition and economic wars between hundreds of factions, guilds, and leagues (whether official, independent, or pirate).

Right: Joe Lee aka BANZAï is the infamous lunatic and suicidal old gambler of the Exodus (the Meliès F.C. league). At the age of 114 he finally decided to switch to a more attractive body, as he was starting to rot. This fact has never gotten in the way of him continuing to seduce young ladies, though.

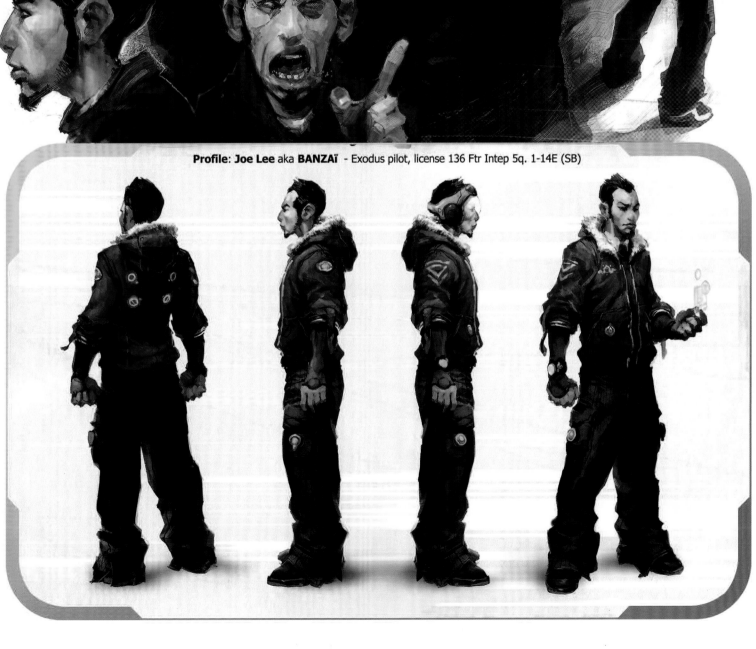

Profile: Joe Lee aka **BANZAï** - Exodus pilot, license 136 Ftr Intep 5q. 1-14E (SB)

02 Department by **Feerik**

Air Force E.P. intervention unit by **Barontieri**

Wandering troops by **Rainart**

HUMAN STRUCTURES

Barontieri: Cities on Earth are for the most part decaying and heavily polluted, with rich people having left either for Mars (if legally selected) or living in giant arches and floating islands over the oceans where the air is less toxic.

Above: Spaceships and moodshot by **Barontieri**
Middle: Urban take off, speedpainting by **Feerik**
Right: Moodshot by **Rainart,** some tall, decaying concrete buildings bathing in the warm sun. The feeling of distress was inspired by a Brazilian industrial landscape.

EARTH CITIES

Barontieri: *"The classic sci-fi theme of the growing gap between social classes is stronger than ever in our story, as we weren't looking for something totally original to start Harry's journey through space and time."*

Right: Glass Museum in downtown, new L.A.
Bottom: Old Montreal's Harbor-Astroport area

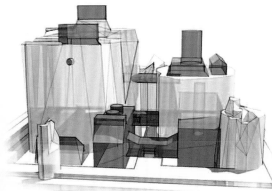

1 - E.P. Headquarters: *"Unit 12 and 6, the suspect has been seen at the Arch 3, zone 57 Terrace C. I repeat..."*

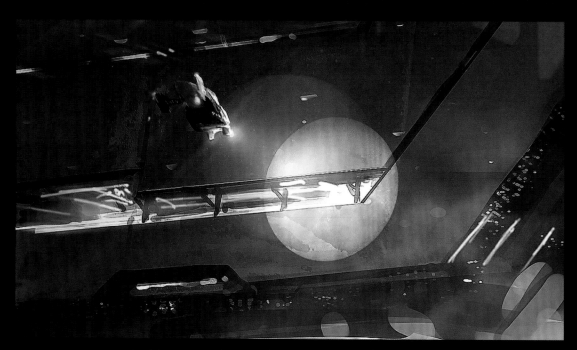

2 - E.P. Unit 12, pilot: *"Gotcha Harry! All units! I have a visual..."*

3 - E.P. Unit 12, sergeant: *"Ground unit steady! Suspect is running toward you!"* Harry is smiling...

ARCHEON

Rainart: *"The concept of this Arch-type building is certainly the oldest one in this book; in fact, it was even made before the project Exodessey began. At first, the Arch was a kind of 'nano-technological' gigantic monument. The idea behind it was an assembling of billions of little cubes with procedural variations on their sizes and positions. Following the first draft, we tried several other iterations before this final version.* **Barontieri** *did a paintover and added the covering structure, the sunset atmosphere, and the glass window; in the meantime I was doing some compositing, matte paintings, and camera mapping tests. We didn't really know which direction to take, and we finally forgot this image until a few years later. When we started to write the story of the book, the Arch eventually found its own place".*

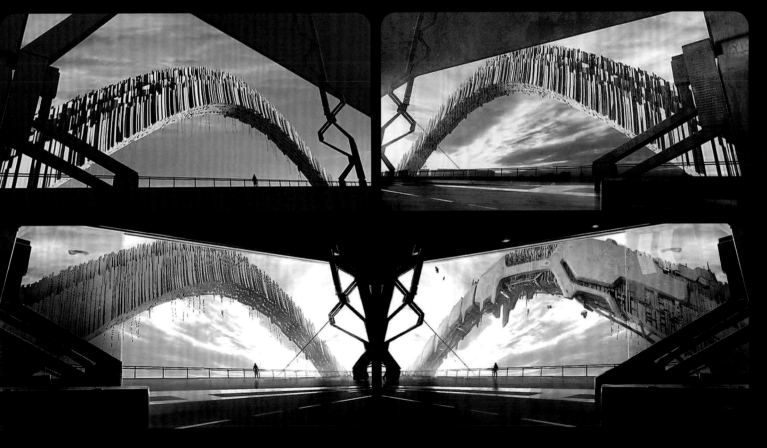

Left page: Storyboard by **Barontieri.** Right page: By **Rainart**

WANTED
FUGITIVE

MALE
WHITE
HEIGHT: 6'7"
WEIGHT: 180 LBS
MEDIUM BUILD
BLACK HAIR
DARK-RED
CYBERNETIC EYES

LAST KNOW ADRESS:
76 CENTRALIS, BLOCK 4, EARTH
12BN-447B9
CALLERS REMAIN ANONYMOUS

URBAN PERSPECTIVES

Top: The Red Columns by **Rainart.**
Above: Machinery by **Vyle**

Rainart: *The RED COLUMNS is a concept for a matte painting. These pillars form a monolithic complex erected more than 500 years ago. I've used Zbrush to sculpt the columns and Photoshop to polish the final image. Eventually, I decided to use it for some compositing and camera mapping tests.*

THE ART OF RAINART

DVD

The image above appears in **Rainart's** DVD, in which he demonstrates the techniques that he uses to create environments for the video game and entertainment industries using Adobe Photoshop®, Pixologic ZBrush®, Autodesk Maya®, and EyeOn Fusion®. From speedpainting to matte painting: 2-D/3-D Pproduction pipeline with Sebastien Larroude. The Gnomon Workshop.

Vyle: *"Quietness and pollution. The intense relationship and opposition of beauty despite destruction is an eternal subject for humans. This piece started as a speed-painting, then later was used as a tutorial for the British magazine Imagine FX."*

The air is dry and dusty and the ground is parched, which makes the journey that much longer. Seventeen days in exile, with their hearts full of the fear of getting caught by the E.P. Most of all, the men fear they won't find anything once they reach the GLOG. Harry told us, "The Exodus is rock solid, it's 70 feet long and 35 feet tall. It'll save us all." Honestly, I don't know if we really believe him, but we're still here, following him...

to it. It was also the first time I was drawing Harry in an actual situation, so I did a bunch of try outs before figuring out which attitude I thought he should adopt. I wanted him fierce and wise at the same time. It's really a challenge to coin a character's traits in a couple of frames. Everything is crucial when creating a dramatic situation: there's the lighting, timing, the character's presence in the framing. The story can only be good if you can find the graphic elements that should go with it."

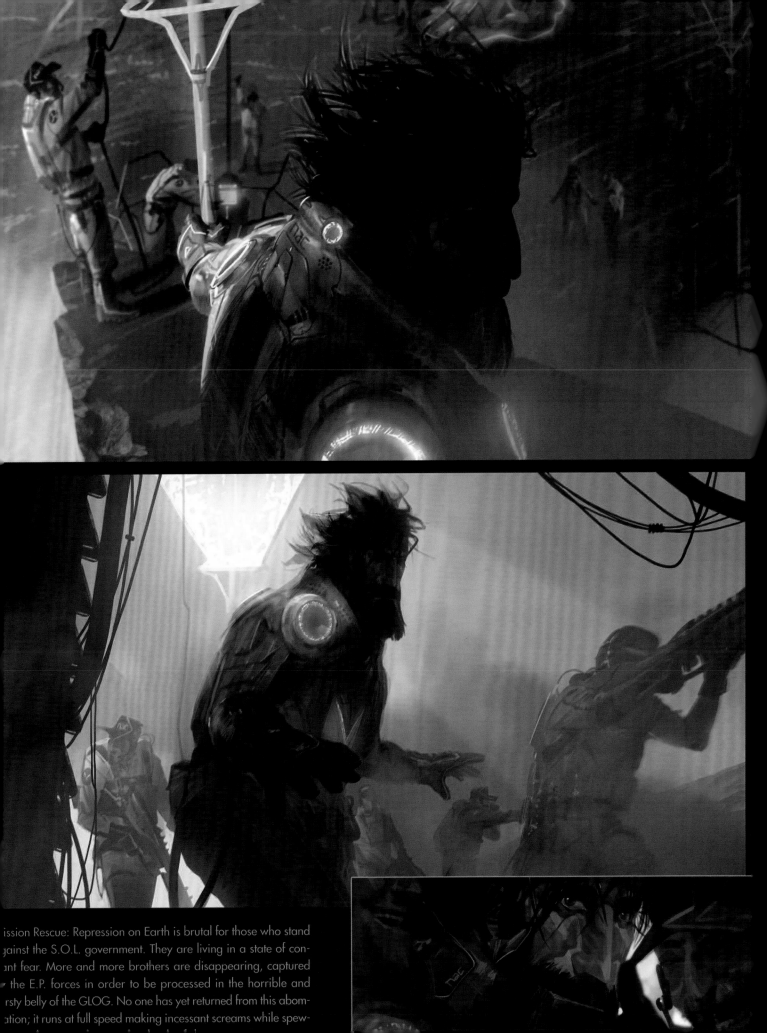

Mission Rescue: Repression on Earth is brutal for those who stand against the S.O.L. government. They are living in a state of constant fear. More and more brothers are disappearing, captured by the E.P. forces in order to be processed in the horrible and thirsty belly of the GLOG. No one has yet returned from this abomination; it runs at full speed making incessant screams while spew-

POLLUSEUM

A combination of two words—"museum" and "pollution." The Polluseum is a giant monument, an elegant shape erected in a no-man's land, a waste zone. It symbolizes the aggressive impulse of human activity on Earth through its phallic design. Image by **Rainart**

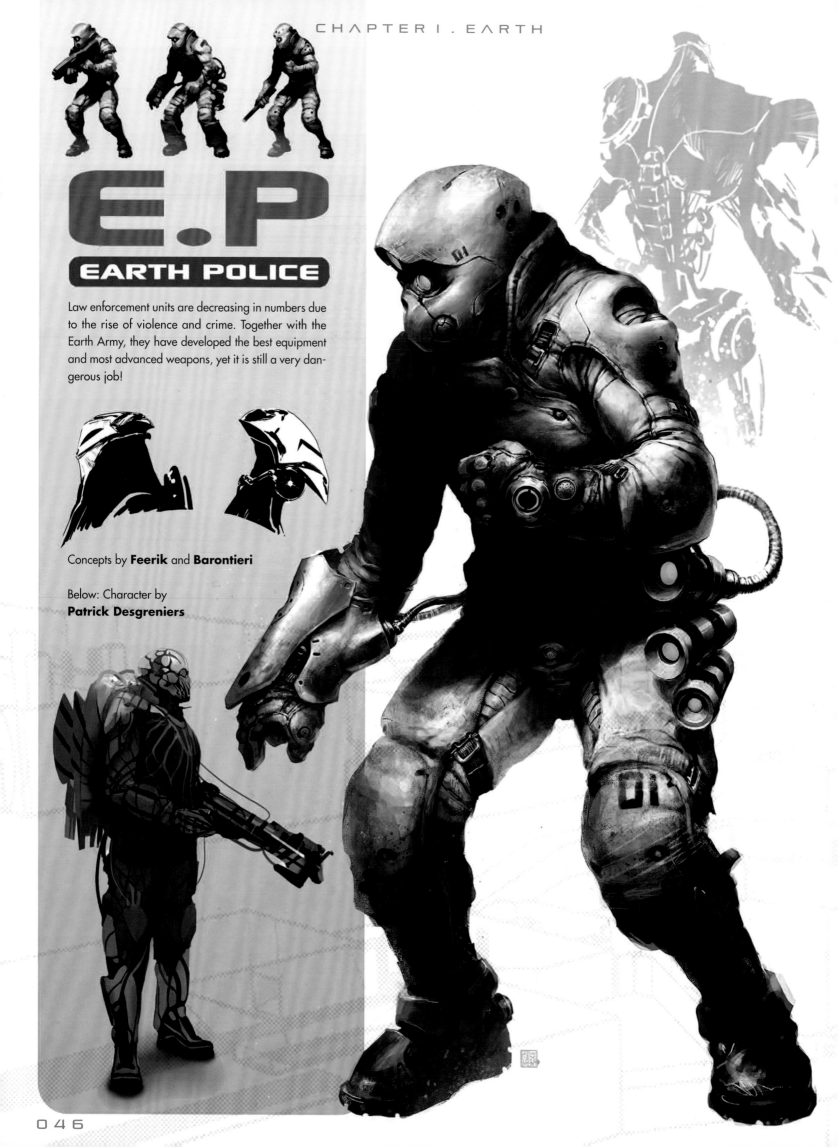

E.P
EARTH POLICE

Law enforcement units are decreasing in numbers due to the rise of violence and crime. Together with the Earth Army, they have developed the best equipment and most advanced weapons, yet it is still a very dangerous job!

Concepts by **Feerik** and **Barontieri**

Below: Character by
Patrick Desgreniers

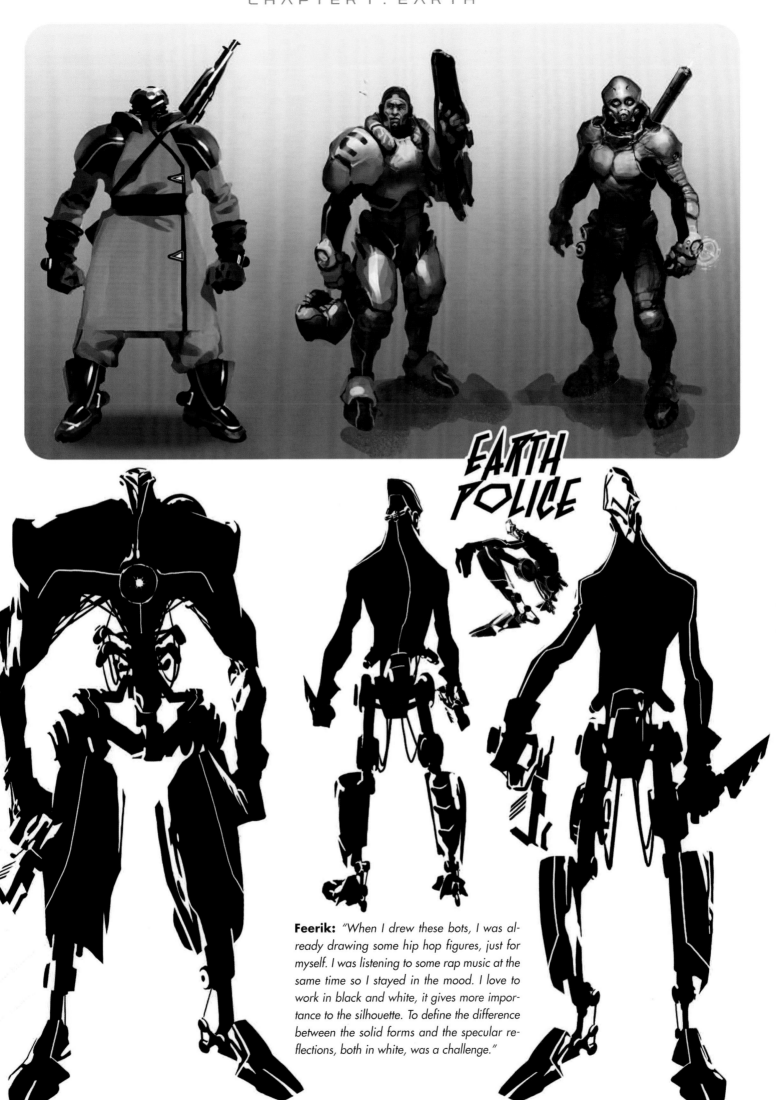

EARTH POLICE

Feerik: *"When I drew these bots, I was already drawing some hip hop figures, just for myself. I was listening to some rap music at the same time so I stayed in the mood. I love to work in black and white, it gives more importance to the silhouette. To define the difference between the solid forms and the specular reflections, both in white, was a challenge."*

Viag: E.P. Forces

TEXTURE AND COLORS

Above and top: Character design by **Patrick Desgreniers**
Top right: Speedpainting by **Barontieri**
Bottom page: Speedpainting by **Feerik**

REFUGEE CAMP

Left page: Chasing refugees (top) by **Barontieri** and storyboard by **Feerik**
Above: Speedpainting by **Feerik**, spaceship design by **Patrick Desgreniers**

Design by Patrick Desgreniers

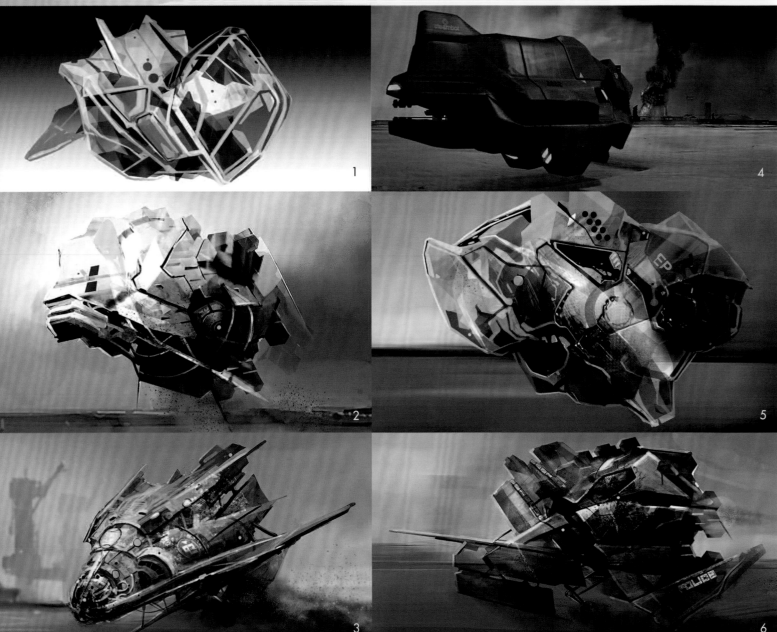

E.P. MOBILE PATROL VEHICLES

Vyle: "Early and final concepts (1, 4, and 5) for the Earth Police ships. Matte armor-skin texturing similar to a dark rubber to avoid reflections, massive opening in the back for military troops and transport deliveries, high-velocity engines." Above 2, 3, and 6: E.P. spaceship designs by **Viag**

Sketches (above) by **Feerik,** color concepts by **Patrick Desgreniers**

Mobilab by **Rainart**, a meteo-ship that measures atmospheric data on the field.

Top: E.P. Troop armored transport ship by **Barontieri**
Left: E.P. multitask spaceship and 3-D models by **Vyle**

E.P. LOADER SERIES

3-D base mesh by **Vyle**

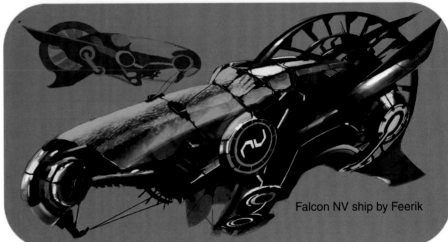

Falcon NV ship by Feerik

VEHICLE DESIGN

Vyle: *"The Earth Police ship is a melting pot of contemporary military vehicles. One of my biggest concerns was to ensure consistent vision by the team throughout. Thanks to previous concepts from **Viag** and **Barontieri,** I created a final version by connecting it as much as possible to a decrepit vision of Earth. The 3-D mesh was built for a matte-painting demo by **Rainart.**"*

1 through 4, top and middle of page by **Patrick Desgreniers.**

Personal vehicle by **Vyle**

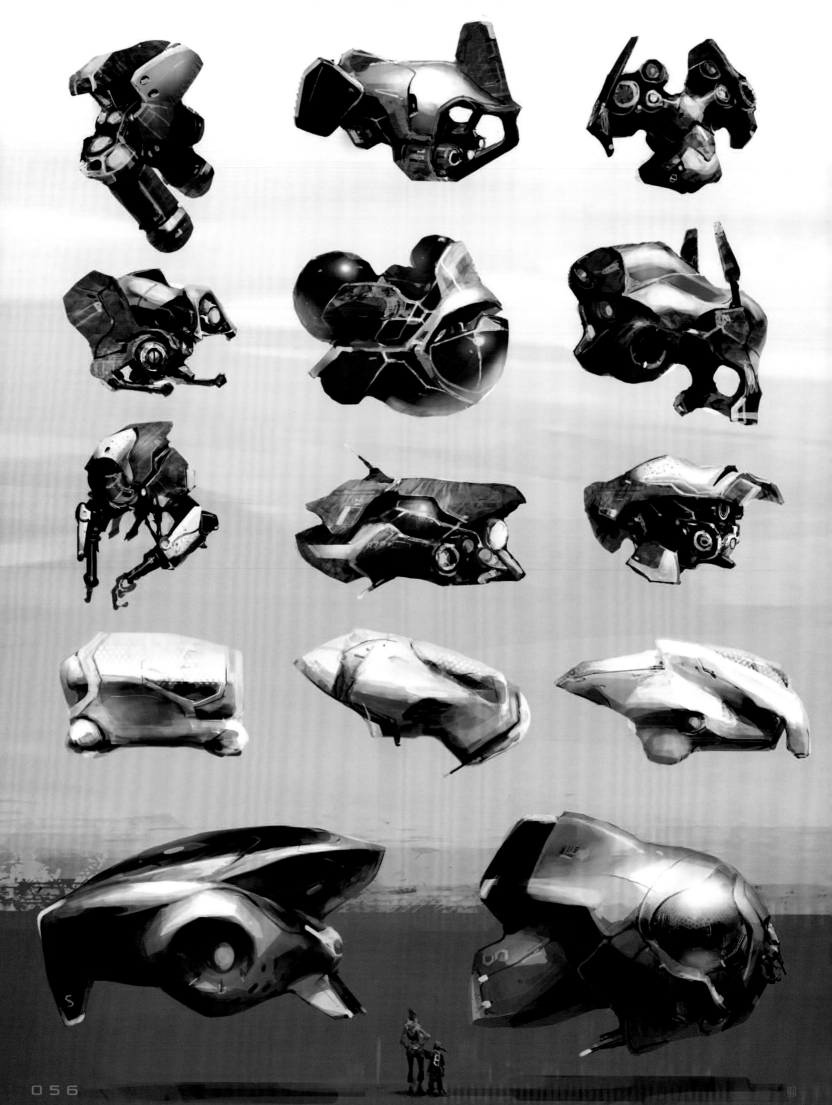

Left: **Barontieri.** Right: **Feerik**

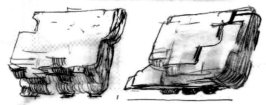

Patrick Desgreniers's drawings

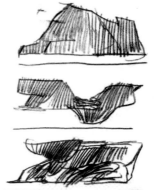

MOTHERSHIPS

This page: "Big Mama" is the nickname given to the Emperor's favorite ceramic vessel. It is powerful enough to travel within the entire S.O.L. territory without recharging its power cells. Designed by **Patrick Desgreniers**

Right page: Motherships by **Viag** where he has tried to create large and heavy shapes, very industrial and believable. Those spaceships can transport thousands of passengers during long trips. He took some visual inspiration from cruise ships, submarines, and airships/blimps.

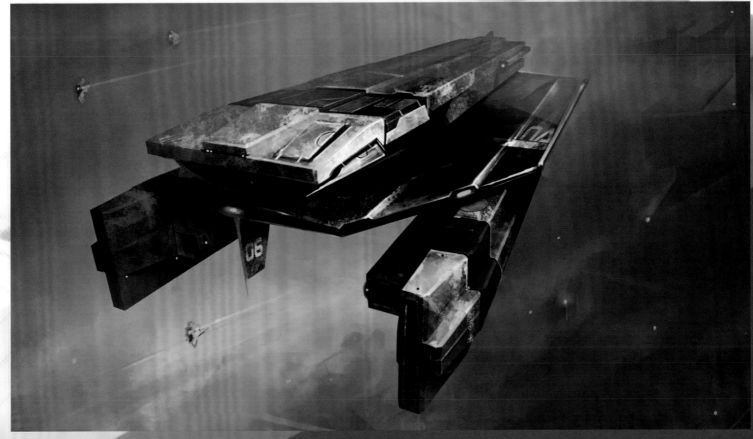

BARONTIERI + FEERIK

//ADAPT 2006 Conference, September 23 and 24, 2006, in Montreal, Canada. **Barontieri:** Speedpainting (1) created along with **Feerik** in an hour-long demo based on a storyboard for the Earth Police attack sequence **Vyle:** Speedpainting (2) created along with **Viag** in an hour-long demo. The last two shots are part of **Rainart's** demo representing STEAMBOT Studios; an animated sequence with an animation of the spaceship by **Mikael Personn.**

The great escape aboard the O.M.I. Shuttles by **Viag**

Vyle: *"This is the first set of sketches created for the Speedpainting to Concept Art Gnomon Workshop DVD. I developed here the concept of 'bubble buildings,' where a microclimate is created in order to protect inhabitants from the pollution of the outside world. The giant gates are also there to protect the downtown area residents who enjoy higher living standards."*

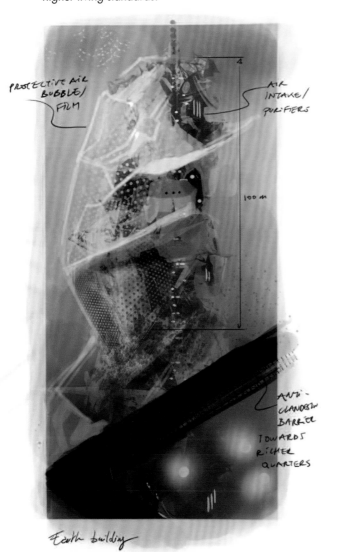

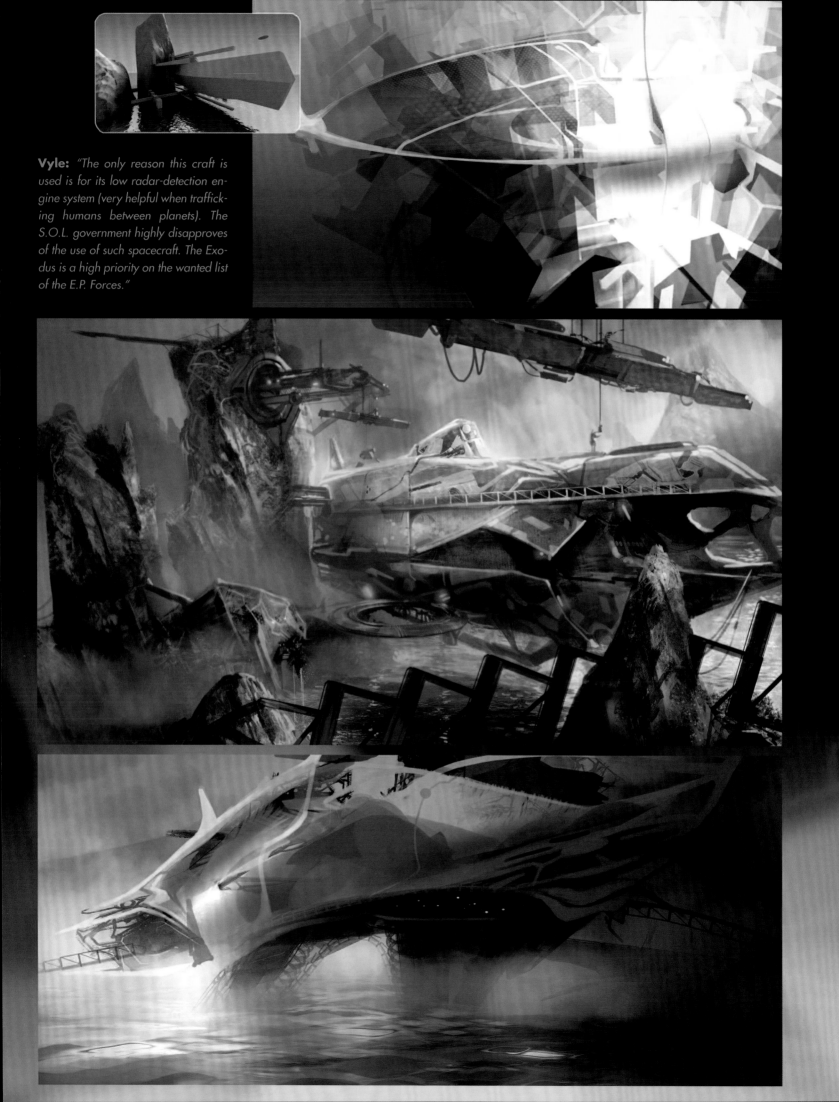

Vyle: *"The only reason this craft is used is for its low radar-detection engine system (very helpful when trafficking humans between planets). The S.O.L. government highly disapproves of the use of such spacecraft. The Exodus is a high priority on the wanted list of the E.P. Forces."*

Sub Pilot Chute MK58—technical files: This spacecraft is probably the least reliable ever conceived. Originally created by the company Abblaim Engines, it failed almost all safety tests, aside from the crash-landing mode. Thanks to its demodulator parts system, it's able to eject all engine and fuel-tank parts in a few milliseconds before crash landing. It is demonstrated here in various modes, including fully inflated "space-bag" bouncers, also called "balloons of pain" by the few people who have survived previous crashes. Its low radar-detection engine system is the only reason why it is so commonly used for human trafficking between planets. The S.O.L. government highly disapproves of the use of such a spacecraft. By **Vyle**

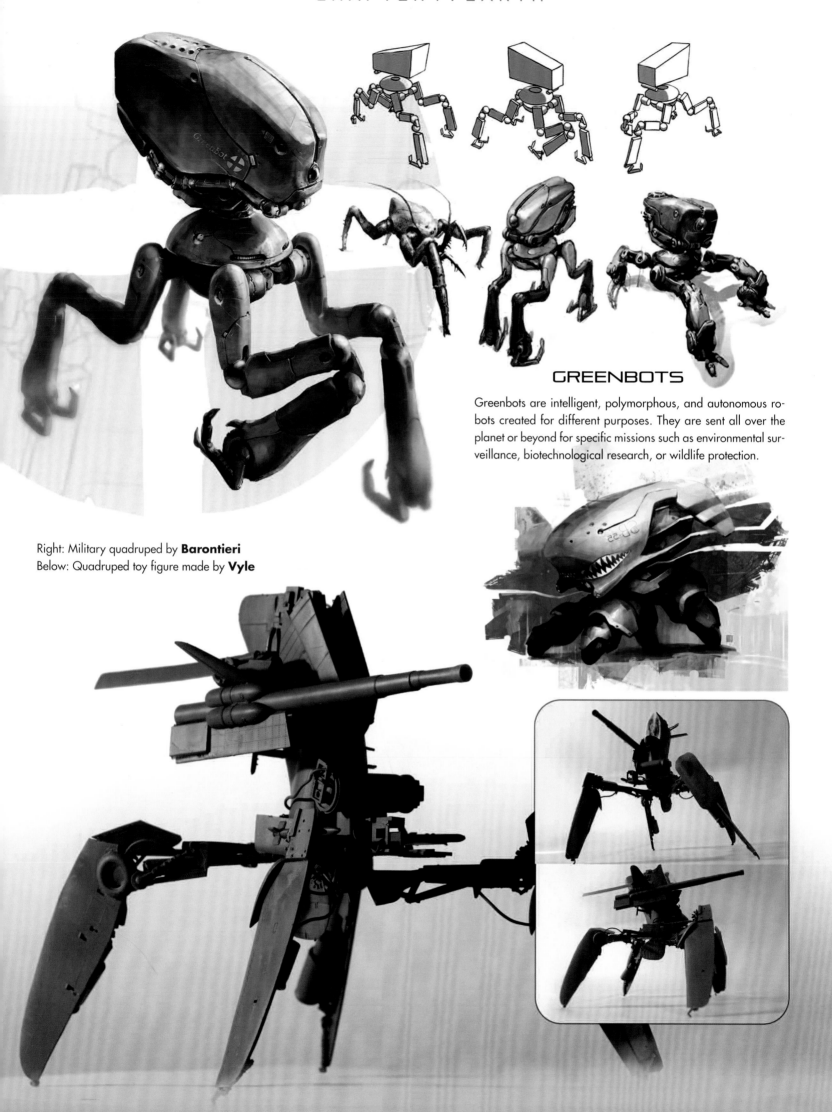

GREENBOTS

Greenbots are intelligent, polymorphous, and autonomous robots created for different purposes. They are sent all over the planet or beyond for specific missions such as environmental surveillance, biotechnological research, or wildlife protection.

Right: Military quadruped by **Barontieri**
Below: Quadruped toy figure made by **Vyle**

PERSONAL TRANSPORTATION

Vyle: *"Despite Earth s state of poverty and disrepair, S.O.L. s ambassadors and important politicians are once in awhile seen aboard luxurious vehicles. Thanks to a particular nano-paint, they do not retain pollution and dust, which allows them to stand out of the traffic in order to emphasize their superiority."*

MOON TRANSFER

… "Repeat. All passengers' seat belts have been locked. All personnel must interface with safety code system D.S.F. Emergency ejection procedure of demodulator pod is now activated...10...9...8..." Harry smiles, he is the only one in position to reach the emergency hatch before it's too late. Good thing he brought his bubble-bag…

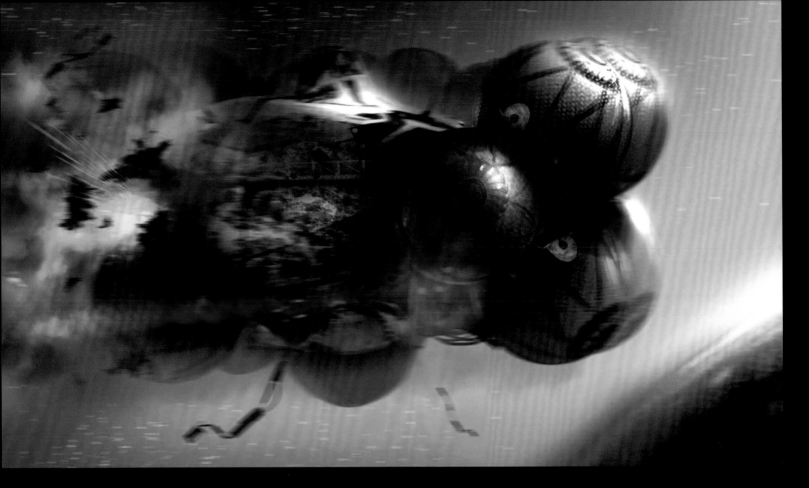

CHAPTER TWO

THE CRASH

The Exodus, victim of an unknown sabotage, finds itself forced to crash land on Earth's old satellite. A few of the crash survivors, including Harry, will end up in low gravity trying to reach one of the famous shield cities covering the Moon's surface. They'll have to find a way to escape the Moon Police Forces, who are always on constant alert. Storyboard: 1, 2, and 3 by **Barontieri** and 4 to 6 by **Vyle.** Animatic test and camera mapping sequence for the Moon, as well as the Exodus crash illustration above by **Vyle.**

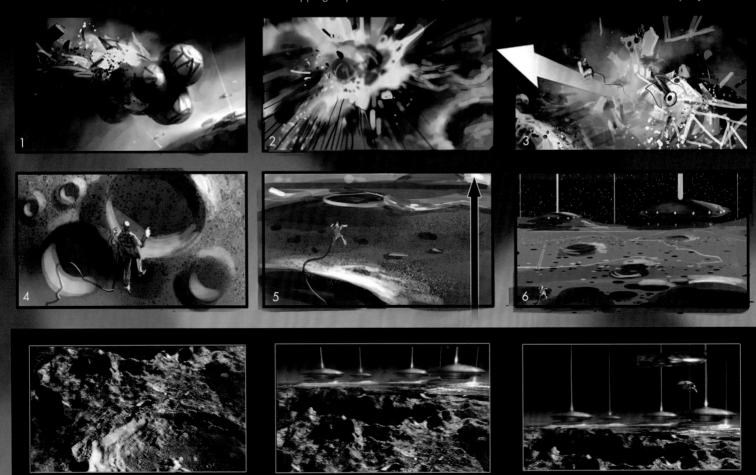

S.O.L. Megaplex Towers by **Vyle**

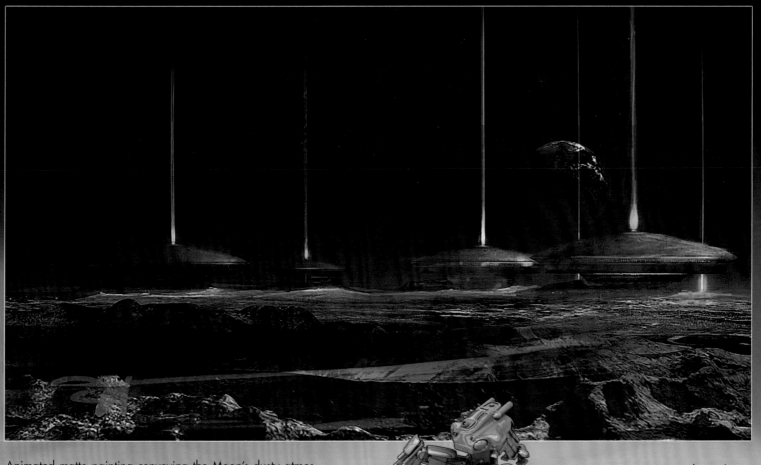

Animated matte painting conveying the Moon's dusty atmosphere, and its typical cities protected by giant "mushroom-like" shields. The original illustration by Vyle was later taken further with a paintover by **Rainart.**

Paintover by **Rainart**

S.O.L. STATION

Moon Astroport is the only S.O.L. station and interface between Earth and Mars. It is an old, rusty place constantly fighting against the harsh Moon dust and destructive solar rays. Life on this desolate sphere is pretty difficult to maintain, and the inhabitants here have the shortest lifespan in our galaxy. However, a lot of activity is still going on here, as in any other border zone. The Astroport is located near Neil Armstrong City (N.A.C.), the capital, which you can see in the background. Only four cities are protected with gigantic shields and are located inside large natural craters.

designed by **Barontieri**

APPOLO MALL

Above: The CRATER is one of the largest leisure centers on the Moon. It has a Biosphere, a lake, and the second largest mall in our solar system. Biosphere concept design by **Rainart** and paintover by **Vyle.**

Left: Astroport, collaboration **Vyle/Feerik**

Barontieri: *"Fire at the drilling platform, level B-12. Exosuit Class XRS often called the 'Chick.' A very common type of working exoskeleton/powersuit on the Moon, which could be used for a large variety of tasks. Safe, efficient, and easy to repair as well as to upgrade makes it a favorite among the space workers."*

RUN 18: REB 3/500 PT

Floating: "Free floating" or "rebound" is an extreme sport involving the use of a bubble-bag to jump from fixed objects and follow a floating course with the lowest possible number of rebounds, while performing complex acrobatics. This spectacular game was invented on the Moon and takes advantage of the planet's unique low-gravity system. Floaters gather around the numerous spots surrounding N.A.C.*, following the official course and Oxygen-Supply-Pipeline Networks (OSPN) with their vital O2-D dispensers.
Concept by **Barontieri.**

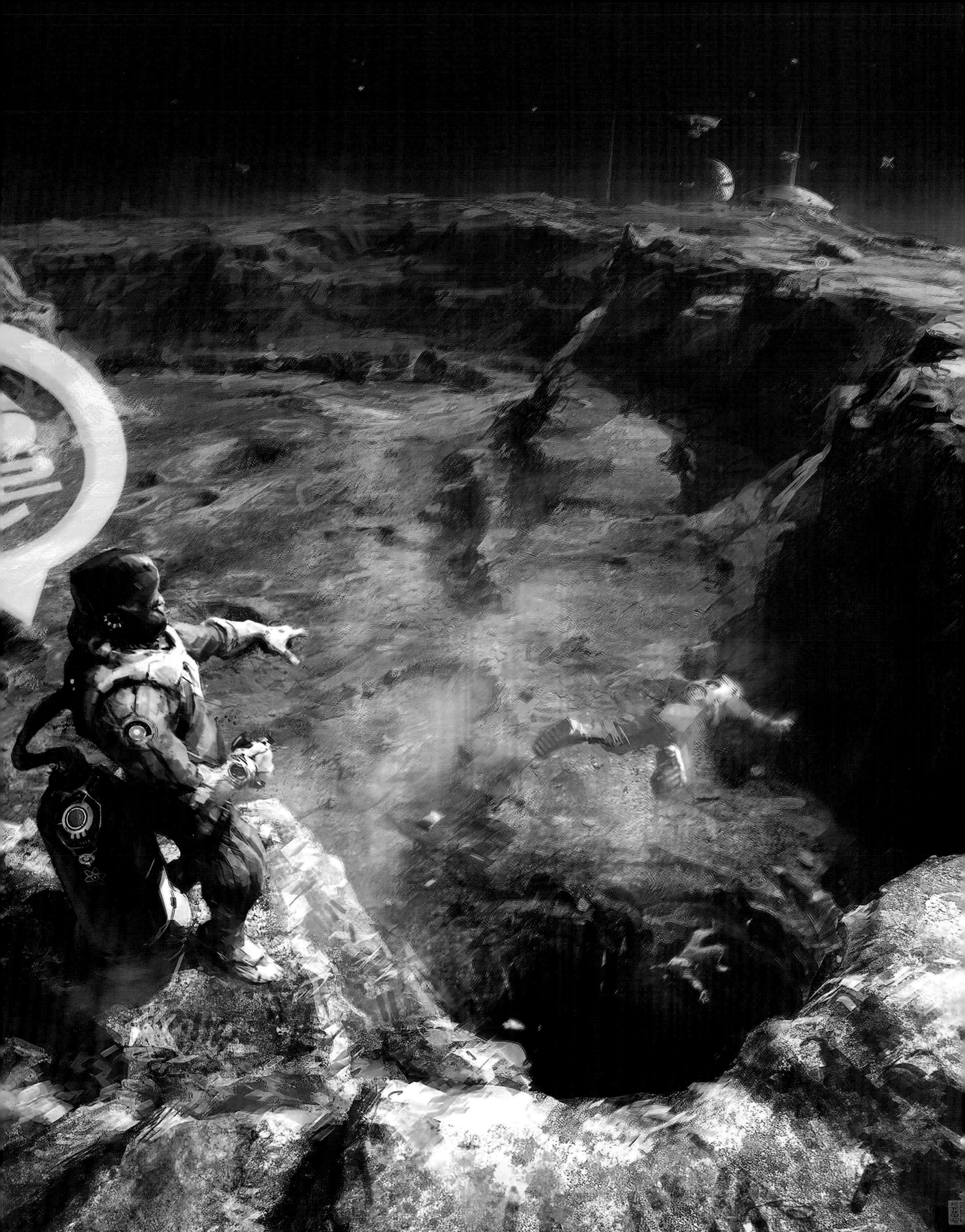

FLOATING

Top: Block-4 Floating training camp, base jump illustration made by Feerik Above: Illegal rebound session from Armstrong City Shield by **Rainart** Left: Floating track by **Barontieri.** Picture an extreme sport that is a mix between golf and skateboarding and you'll get a pretty good idea of what it is!

Feerik: "We figured out a very distinctive way to work with Viag. He creates 3-D models for all the team, and he's really fast. It's a real pleasure to paint over such a cool design, with all the reflections and Global Illumination (GI) separated. We have worked with various 3-D artists in the past and in many cases it was difficult to correctly express our ideas while trying to make sure the artists did not feel walked on! Viag does it wonderfully."

Paintover by **Feerik** **BH-720** series

Moonday

The first lunar express drilling company

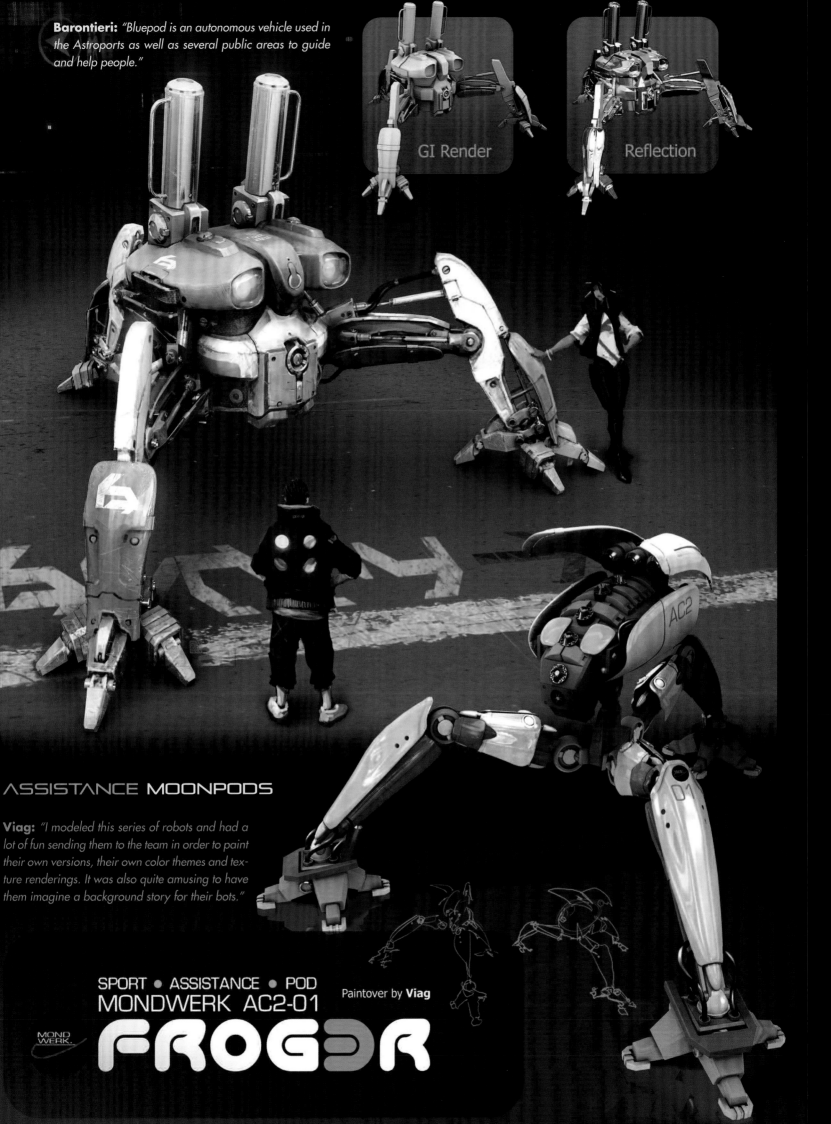

Barontieri: *"Bluepod is an autonomous vehicle used in the Astroports as well as several public areas to guide and help people."*

GI Render

Reflection

ASSISTANCE MOONPODS

Viag: *"I modeled this series of robots and had a lot of fun sending them to the team in order to paint their own versions, their own color themes and texture renderings. It was also quite amusing to have them imagine a background story for their bots."*

SPORT • ASSISTANCE • POD
MONDWERK AC2-01

Paintover by **Viag**

MOND
WERK.

FROG3R

WELCOME TO MARS

...*"Dear passengers, we hope you enjoyed this flight from Moon—N.A.C. to Capital: H³O. The commander of the new Plasma 53 Carrier is proud to have you aboard. Enjoy our Megadome and its tropical temperature (28°C), swim with the fishbots in Gamma Lagoon, relax and drink our famous Tokyo cocktails. Dear future citizens of Mars, it's pleasure tiiiiiiiimel..."*

WELCOME TO MARS
火星へようこそ
BIENVENIDO EN MARZO
欢迎来到火星
BIENVENUE SUR MARS

Above: Mount Olympus by **Barontieri**
Below: Toxic lava by **Rainart**

MARTIAN **RELIEF**

Mars's imagery is far from that of the early 21st century. Thanks to the phenomenon called ter-raforming, and billions of S.O.L.. credits, a fully breathable atmosphere is now available to the colonies. The oceans, artificially created through condensation, allow for the formation of clouds and a deep blue oxygenated sky. Despite numerous problems among the settlers, the red planet is now a very peaceful and rich planet.

Vyle: *"Inspired by one of the 3-D renders created by Rainart (above), I decided to build a
bridge structure holding a mining structure."*

In deserted areas, all is about mining. Mining on Mars has completely un-
balanced Earth's economy and recreated a solar system economy, based entirely on a rich and all-powerful Mars.

Rainart: *"Purple is another mood of the canyon, showing huge monolithic buildings in the desert."*

Rainart: *"GEODESY is a purification station. Mars is still in evolution, that is why the water is treated chemically to be used for various purposes."*

GEODESY Access Corridor, concept by **Feerik**

Rainart: *"Gray is another color variant for the canyon, being less saturated, because of the pollution and terraforming."*

THE GATHERING

Vyle: *"This was the subject of my DVD From Speedpainting to Concept Art. Most of the research was focused on choosing an architectural style for the S.O.L. religious dictatorship. Here, the dictator is greeted on his platform by a group of organized military units. In terms of design, the goal was to create a contrast between the purity of colors and shapes and the actual antihumanistic goals of the S.O.L. organization."*

Dictator's embassy, main image from the DVD

Both pages: Concepts by **Vyle**

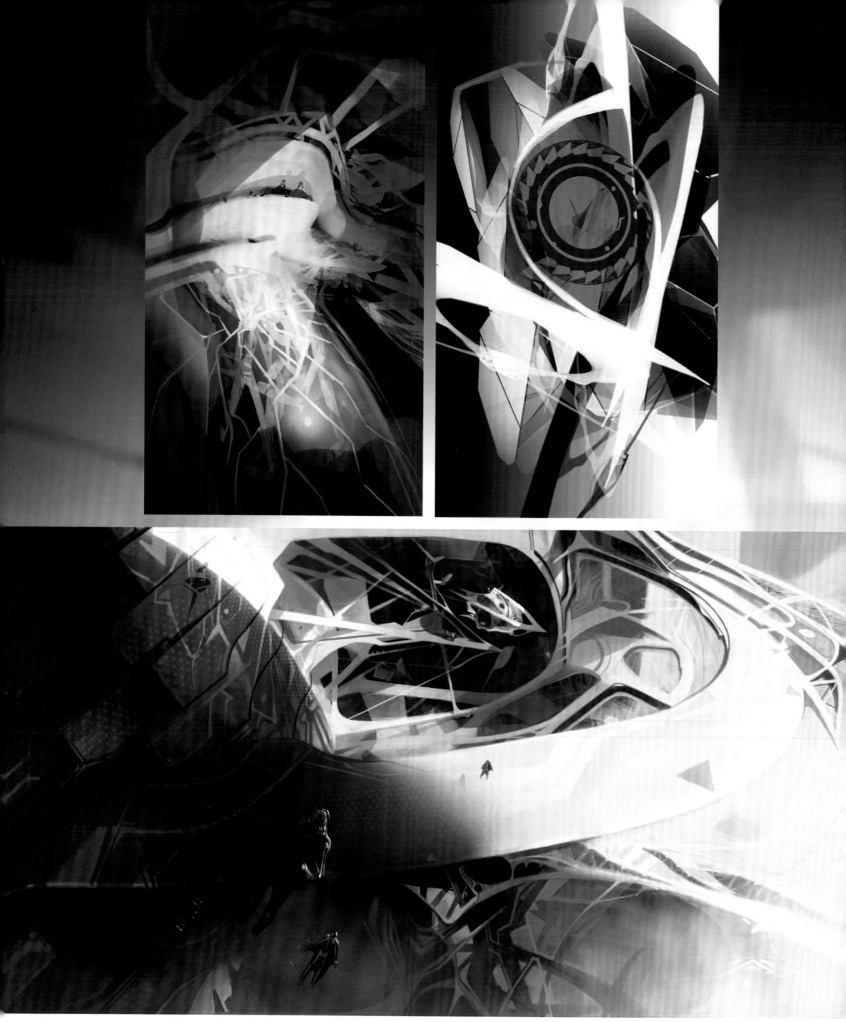

Vyle: *"This is the very first painting ever done for the book. The idea of mixing Halloween and science fiction was the first inspiration for its creation. I'm passionate about wing suits, and this illustration is a mix of all of the above."*

THE EMPEROR'S KINGDOM

Barontieri: *"The Emperor's main palace is located on Mount Olympus and is a megalomaniac, advanced hi-tech structure with a neo-Greek flavor."*

Top: Concepts by **Barontieri**
Left: Sketch by **Vyle**

"There are no rudimentary technologies on Mars. Behind a light, transparent, and simple shape is hidden a complex machinery, like an octopus. Without life, without intelligence, we could not be aware of it."

Here is a prototype of a Martian house based on the valley around Mount Olympus. These flexible houses are spaced far apart in contrast to the over-population of Earth. We wanted something close to ancient Greece, with white walls, pure shapes and Mediterranean cypress trees.

Walls are made of a reflective material, functioning with the solar energy and able to maintain a constant temperature thanks to a yellow roof, without apparent mechanism. Some windows could appear by touching tactile zones, creating a variable transparency across the wall.

Concept by **Barontieri** and **Rainart**

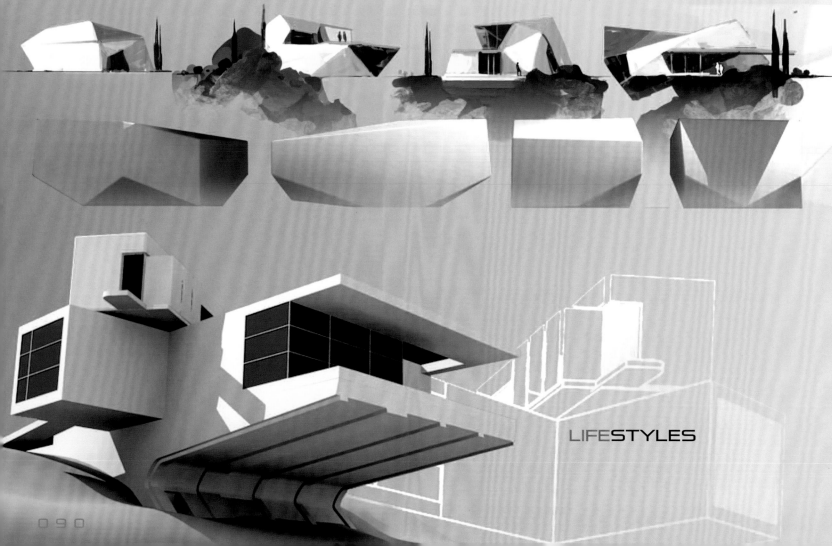

LIFESTYLES

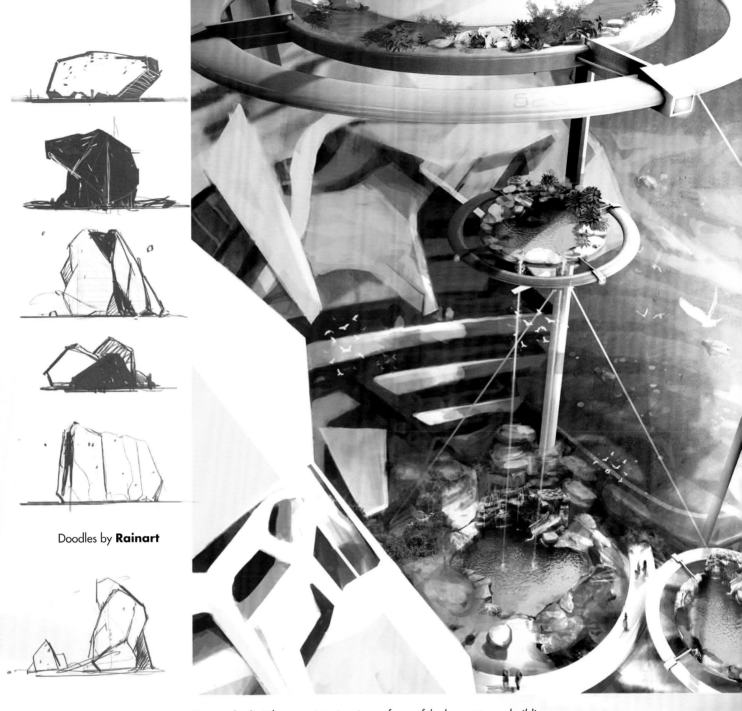

Doodles by **Rainart**

Barontieri: *"These are interior views of one of the largest tower buildings on Mars, which contains apartments, offices, shopping malls, pools, and leisure centers with a large artificial sea."*

MARS

ENJOY AT FULL SPEED! WELCOME TO OUR NEW COLONISTS

LUXURY MANSIONS - NUDRIFT LEAGUE - ARTIFICIAL LAGOONS - SUBURBMARINES

...Enjoy our Megadome and its tropical temperature (28°C), swim with the fishbots in the Gamma Lagoon, relax and drink our famous Tokyo cocktails, enjoying the view on the Mount Olympus.

Top: Concept by **Viag**
Above and left: Concepts by **Vyle**

WELCOME TO MARS

SHOPPING AT MEGADOME

DRINK AT HIROSHIMA COCKTAILS

Storyboards by **Feerik**
Above: Waterfalls by **Barontieri**
Blue Lagoon by **Simonak**

GAMMA LAGOON

ACHILLES MENAUPHIS, EMBASSADOR OF MARS

Concepts by **Patrick Desgreniers**

HARRY (360°)

HARRY turnarounds. Concepts by **Barontieri**

Left side
Back
Right side

Scale : —
Weight : ~ 75 Kg
Height : ~ 1,80 M

DVD

P.A.R.T.One
Notes :

- Right side > See. Helmet
- Facial expressions
> See. Harry_Face_01
- Equipment and suit details
> See. Harry_Details_01

STEAMBOT Studios Inc. | Harry (casual suit) | — / 06 / 07

▶ HARRY SUITV2

When Harry eventually arrives on Mars and is deported to Valles Marineris, he is a different man with a brand new look. In order to escape the Martian customs officers, he has undergone a light surgical procedure in N.A.C. His new V2 suit (impact nanoderm technology) is essential to help him survive in the VMMC Mines.

■ HARRY: SD

"Research, expression board, and model sheet created for the Gnomon Workshop tutorial DVD, Character Design Pipeline: Production Art & Research Techniques, with **BARONTiERi.***"*

Top left: Concept by **Patrick Desgreniers**

Top right: Concept by **Vyle**

Below: Concepts for the Martian Cydolls by **Barontieri** and **Feerik**

cydoll
4 love...

AKIKO ROGER

Akiko "Ghost" Roger is an elite S.O.L. pilot, a double agent who once infiltrated the most dangerous space pirate gang, Jollyrouge. At 58, she is considered one of the best pilots in the galaxy and has won the Medal of Honor. She met Harry back on Earth when she helped capture some pirates. Their relationship has been quite hectic and dramatic since then. Now they'll have to cooperate during the Samhuinn mission.

Concept by **Barontieri**

SOL AMBASSADOR   TRAITOR/ESCAPE   MISSION CONTROL   MARS/SABOTAGE

THE FIRST CREW

...A group of astronauts who have nothing to lose, the so-called "defenders of the enlightened truth" (a complete media manipulation of S.N.N.), is put together in order to solve the mystery behind the supernatural appearances happening all over the solar system.

Technical lead, Lou "Boss" Bouma—a colonel with a mysterious past and a former astrophysicist—and Ambassador Puhell...

Concepts by **Vyle**

"Doctor Weklan"
Cyborg Class.eM
(Empathy Medical Class)

Barontieri: *"I wanted the scientist to appear as the most "human" person from the crew, despite being almost entirely cybernetic (Cyborg Type A). Doc is an easy going, funny, naïve, and emotional being. I started with a classic cold-hearted archetype of a sci-fi doctor but finally ended up with a more original character."*

DOC
CLASS CYBORG/TYPE A
MOHAMED ASKLEPIUS 142 Y.O/OLYMPUS CITY

01   02   03   04

HARMONY PURITY

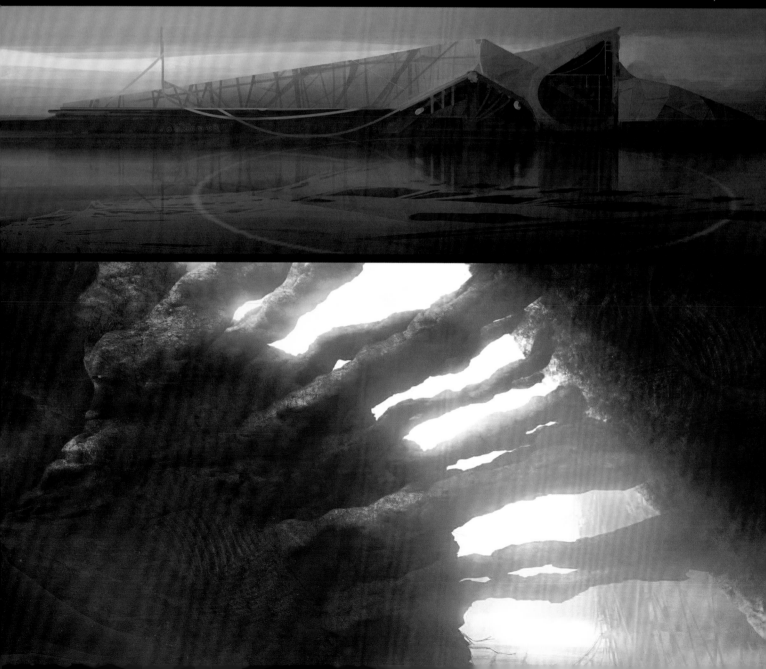

...Mars seems to be an idyllic world where nature regains its rights. This is a perfect balance between the terraforming and the ecosystem. The nano-cubes are still growing in the desert lands, producing all the water that the ground, plants, and humans need. Since the first colonization, Martian inhabitants have developed a unique technology, respecting life cycles and seasons, recycling energy, and preserving life...

THE FIRST PIONEERS

Mars has finally been terraformed after decades of intense work by a myriad of robots preparing for the arrival of the first human colony. Phase 1 was a success. The colonization of the red planet began even without a fully breathable atmosphere. The first pioneers spread rapidly and soon started the construction of Olympus Mon to celebrate the official entry of their new planet into the S.O.L.

Top: Concept by **Patrick Desgreniers,** thumbnail by **Rainart**
Above: The desert lands by **Barontieri**
Left: Concept by **Rainart**

Top: First steps on the red planet, concept by **Feerik**
Right: Paintover by **Barontieri/Rainart**
Below: Nano-technological structures, concept by **Rainart**

Top: Paintover by **Rainart** based on **Vyle's** concept (middle)
Above: Concepts by **Vyle**

...The Valles Marineris Mines Corp. is a private company that owns the most beautiful canyon in the S.O.L. universe. They are managing both the mines (30 percent of the domain) and the national park (70 percent is a public but protected area)...

...The Valles Marineris Mines Corp. is a private company that owns the most beautiful canyon in the S.O.L. universe. They are managing both the mines (30 percent of the domain) and the national park (70 percent is a public but protected area)...

Paintover by **Barontieri** based on a **Rainart's** concept

Vyle: *"This is a medium-sized quadruped, used mostly for group transportation in between mining stations."*

Opposite page: VMMC Mines concept by **Barontieri**
Top: Mines activity, concept by **Feerik**
Middle left: Concept by **Simonak**
Middle right: Concept by **Simonak**
Left: Mines foreman, designed by **Feerik**

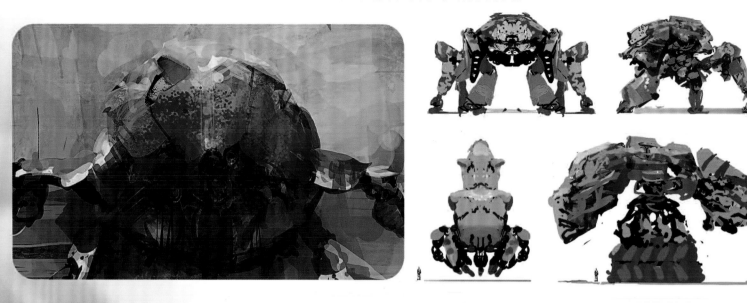

Both pages: Concepts by **Patrick Desgreniers**

THE PURSUIT

Harry is fleeing from the Crabb. The giant mechanical digger is after him because of a serious malfunction in its A.I. device—at least that is what the official report published by the construction site police concluded. The State Department had noticed our hero's braveness and audacity and decided to assign him to a secret mission. In order to erase his identity from federal records, they had to fake his death by staging an assassination. With Harry off the map, the Department is able to take him away to Crater 33, where he will receive training and instructions for his next assignment.

Feerik: *"Research for mining robots."*

Barontieri: *"You can see several ideas for some of the Martian robots on this double-page spread. Research paintovers for CET done by **Vyle** (red) and **Rainart** above."*

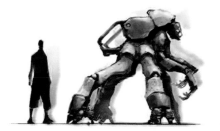

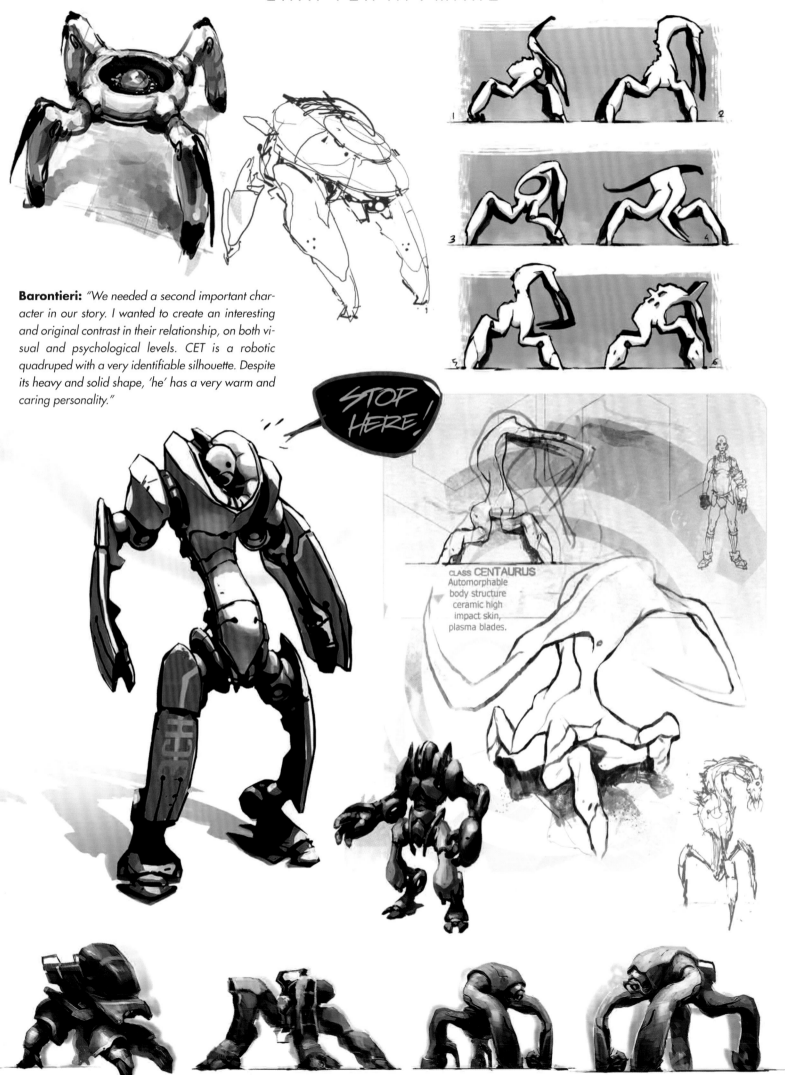

Barontieri: *"We needed a second important character in our story. I wanted to create an interesting and original contrast in their relationship, on both visual and psychological levels. CET is a robotic quadruped with a very identifiable silhouette. Despite its heavy and solid shape, 'he' has a very warm and caring personality."*

STOP HERE!

CLASS **CENTAURUS**
Automorphable
body structure
ceramic high
impact skin,
plasma blades.

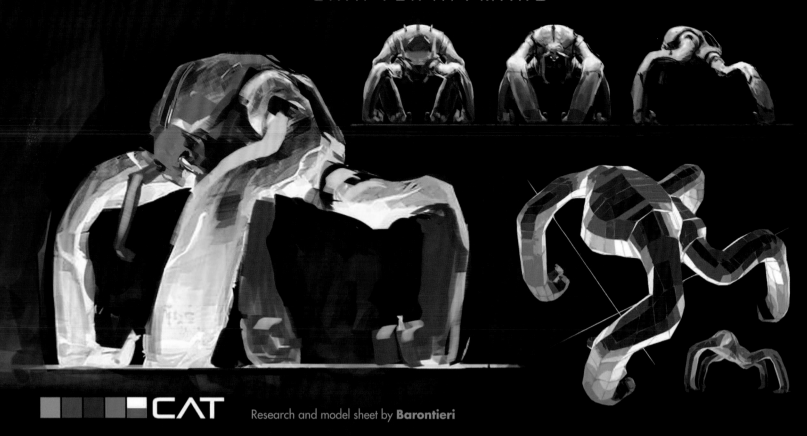

■■■■■CAT Research and model sheet by **Barontieri**

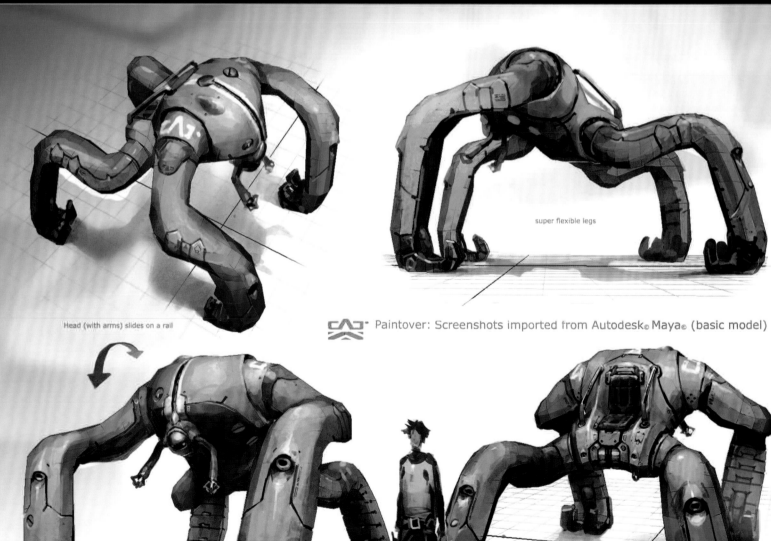

Head (with arms) slides on a rail

super flexible legs

CAT Paintover: Screenshots imported from Autodesk© Maya© (basic model)

Rescue seat (back)

P.A.R.T ONE
PRODUCTION ART & RESEARCH TECHNIQUES

BARONTIERI

THE GNOMON WORKSHOP

STEAMBOT

Barontieri: Final presentation board showing Harry and CET having a good time in the VMMC Mines.

Vyle: *"Ananta Sun, Harry, and CET escape the mines and plan on climbing in order to establish communication with a rescue ship."*

Feerik: *"Now in a safe place, our heroes get some rest in the heights of Mount Olympus."*

THE POLAR EXPEDITION

Rainart: *"The team continues to climb the polar cap in search of these 'ghost appearances' detected from the S.O.L. station. This is the first time that Harry hears about these strange and scary encounters*

NANO-ARTIFACTS

Rainart: *"It has been awhile since the nano-modules relied on humans to function. Depending on the environmental pressure, some of them disappear to let other faster and smarter ones take over. They occasionally leave behind some strange residual shapes, creating mysterious geometric forests here to stay forever—those are called nano-cubes. Some of the inhabitants know how to harvest the cubes. The nano-oasis is also very dear to the heart of the mercenaries, as these surroundings are very unstable and dangerous."*

Original concept made in Photoshop.
The snowy version was part of an animated sequence composited in Digital Fusion.

Feerik: *"This is the fusion of Rainart's highway concept (below) and Simonak's vehicle designs (next pages). We have been huge fans of the video games F-Zero and WipEout for a few years now, so we thought it would be fun to create our own take on it. But we wanted something more dirty and brutal than a clean techno-look, something a bit closer to Mad Max. I even imagined some logos, decals, and visuals for the league, in the event that we wanted to push the concept further.*

ENTER THE RACE

...In order to be included in the "Halloween Mission," Harry has to show off his talents during an incredible but perilous form of racing called Nudrift, where hotheaded pilots clash on the Martian highways while going over a 1000 mph,. For him, this is not just the most popular show on Mars— becoming one of these pilots is his dream.

Above: Martian highway by **Rainart**
Left and right: The race by **Feerik**

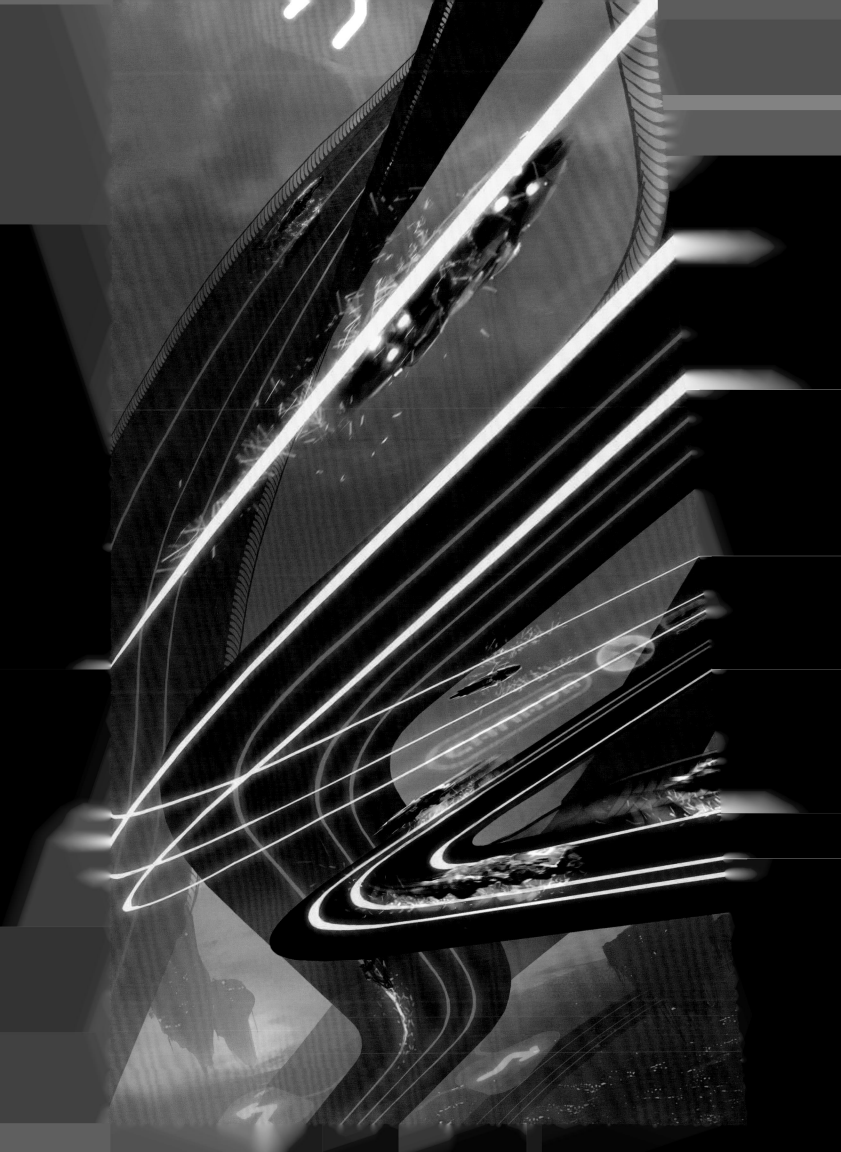

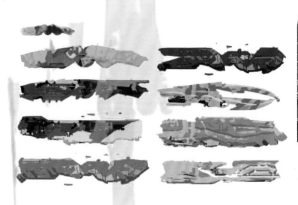

NUDRIFT
JUST BRING YOUR BALLS™

Patrick: _"During a life-drawing session, the model was hidden by some people in front of me. So I decided to discreetly paint those watercolors of Nudrift racers (below) while nobody was watching. So I only spent 15 minutes on it."_

Both pages: Concepts by **Patrick Desgreniers**

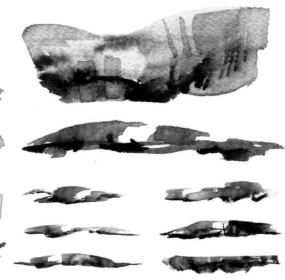

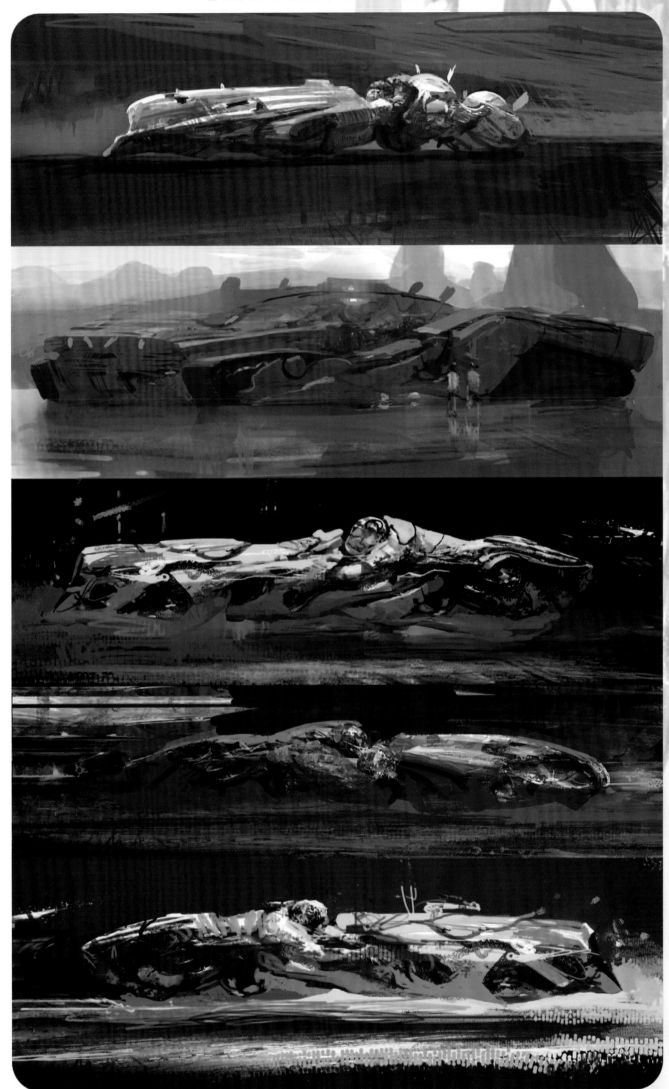

NUDRIFT™
official martian racing league

Efficient Technology has started working on Mars for the army, as they were asked by the Department of Defense to build non-polluting engines in order to ensure we would not repeat the same mistakes that were made on Earth. After four years of research, Red Division's first Nudrift military model was produced. The anti-gravity engine, running on a Compensatory Energy System (C.E.S.), was born. Six months later, Joe Zellenberg, the physicist who invented the system, disappeared. There were a number of rumors about how he had been kidnapped, but none of them were actually based on hard facts. Efficient Technology eventually developed an entire range of vehicles to be sold to the population of Mars. This led to the creation of a professional racing team, and that is how the Mars Elite Championship became a national sport on Mars.

3-D model by **Viag**, paintover on 3-D by **Feerik**

Patrick Desgreniers: *"I've always been a great fan of WipEout, so I designed a compact anti-gravity monospace vehicle. A shell closes around the pilot when the engine starts and ensures that the pilot doesn't get ejected when taking curves at high speeds. A simple pressure of the annular finger can control the inclination of the monospace. In the event of a crash, a protective sphere surrounds the pilots to prevent major injuries."*

WORMHOLE DIVING

"At least," thought Harry just before his body was stretched to infinity, "I am enjoying quite an amazing sight!"
During the very first test with Harry as a guinea pig, he tumbles towards the wormhole gate at immeasurable speeds, then everything seems to go awry. After a temporal shockwave stronger than the others, the ship's structural integrity collapses on itself and bounces our hero into the void. Among titanium ship parts, distorted like noodles by the incredible wormhole pres-

CHAPTER FOUR

INFINITY SKIES SERIES **VMK-8**   *BLACKHOLE AERO SUIT*

Feerik: *"Conceived especially for Harry, the VMK-8 is equipped with the very latest innovations in terms of ergonomics, security, resistance, comfort, elasticity, pressurization, and anti-corrosion. This latest molded fibro-titanium model withstands a pressure of 8Gs."*

Concepts by **Feerik**

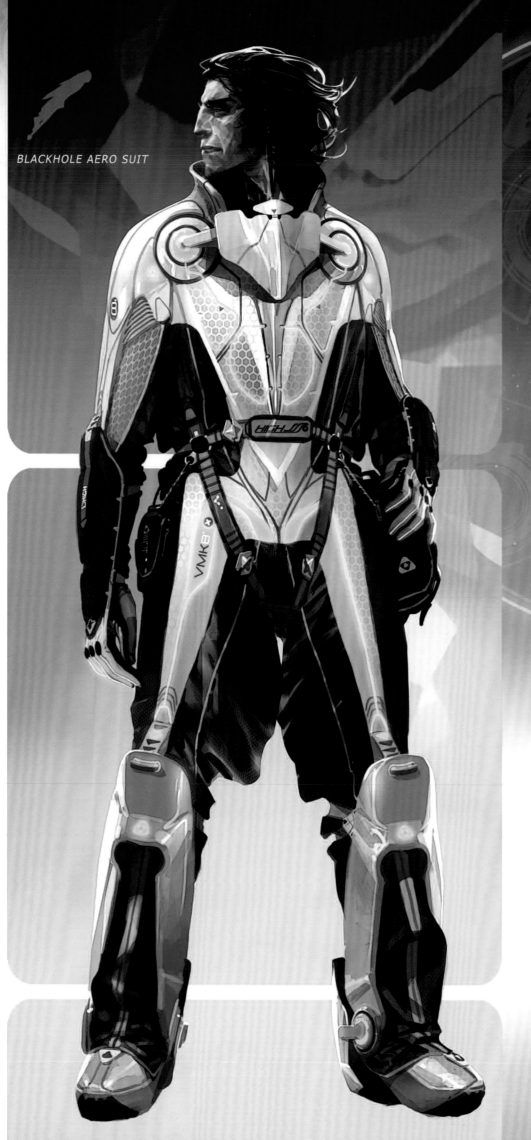

This page: Concepts by **Vyle**

WORMHOLE LAUNCH STATION

This is the only space station in the solar system that can reliably launch ships towards a fairly precise point on the other side of our galaxy. Here are some of the test ships.

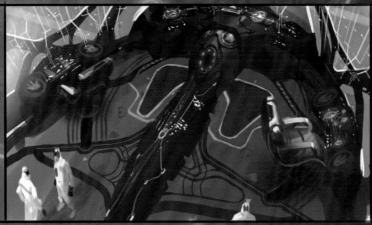

BLACKHOLE EXPERIMENTAL GO2 STATION

Developed especially for the purpose of discovering what is happening beyond the Martian Gamma System (GO2). The scientists believe in another life form, more complex and unique. They believe in SAMHUINN.

This page: Concepts by **Feerik**

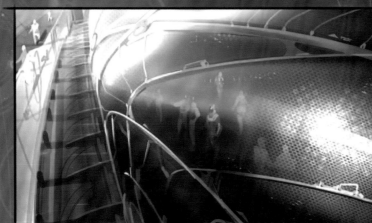

SAY GOODBYE

Now is the time to say "goodbye." Everything is ready for take off.
From control station to gates securing, everything is under control.

This page: Concepts by **Vyle**

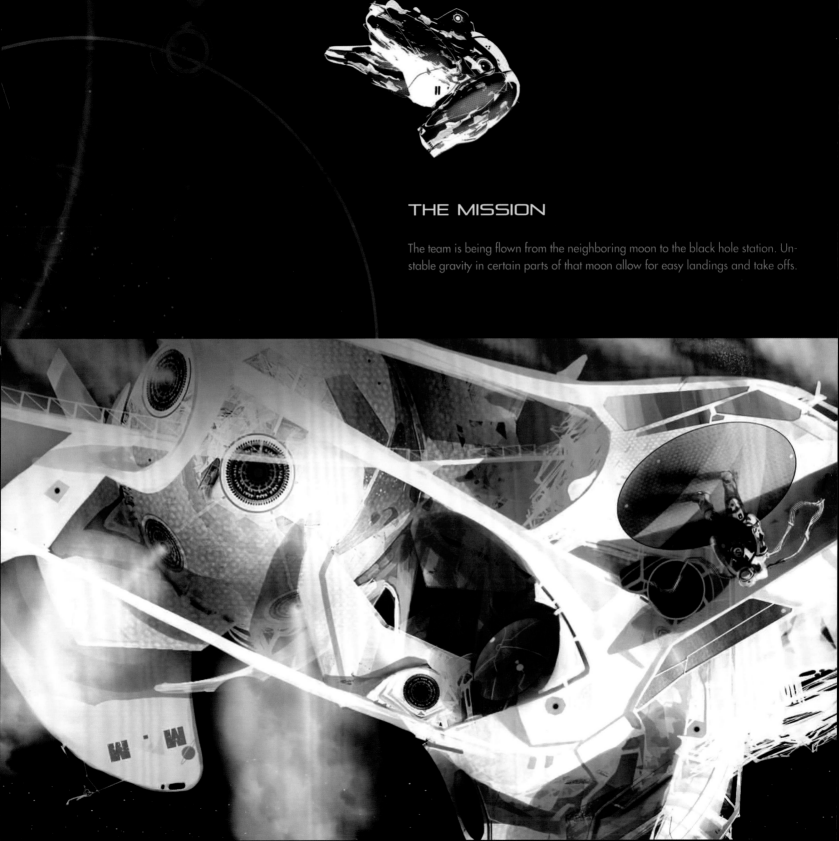

THE MISSION

The team is being flown from the neighboring moon to the black hole station. Unstable gravity in certain parts of that moon allow for easy landings and take offs.

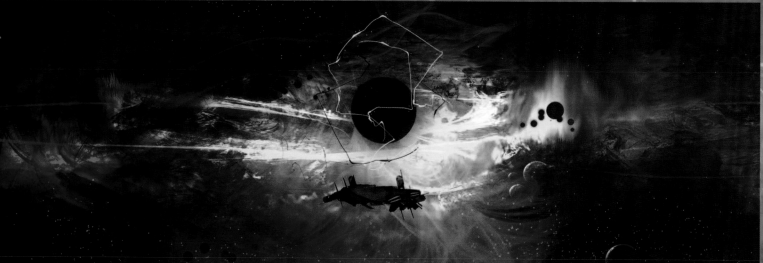

This page: Concepts by **Vyle**

THE PROBE

Rainart: *"THOT is a space spy probe. In the vicinity of the black hole, it is still and listening, analyzing, and scanning for any molecular changes. It is independent and self-sufficient. Its form is a geometric opposition of two shapes: a circle (Deus, the unknown, nothingness, after), and a cube or rectangle (a human creation). I named the probe THOT after the Egyptian God known as the "Lord of Time."*

Top: Concepts by **Vyle**
Left: Concept by **Rainart**

SAMHUINN

Dark pioneers of the cosmos are forgotten and doomed to a long journey with their scary suits, creepy vehicles, and odd rituals because they need to remember this journey, the failure, and the pain. They need to remember how they became strong through death and fear, to become that which is to be feared.

CHAPTER FIVE

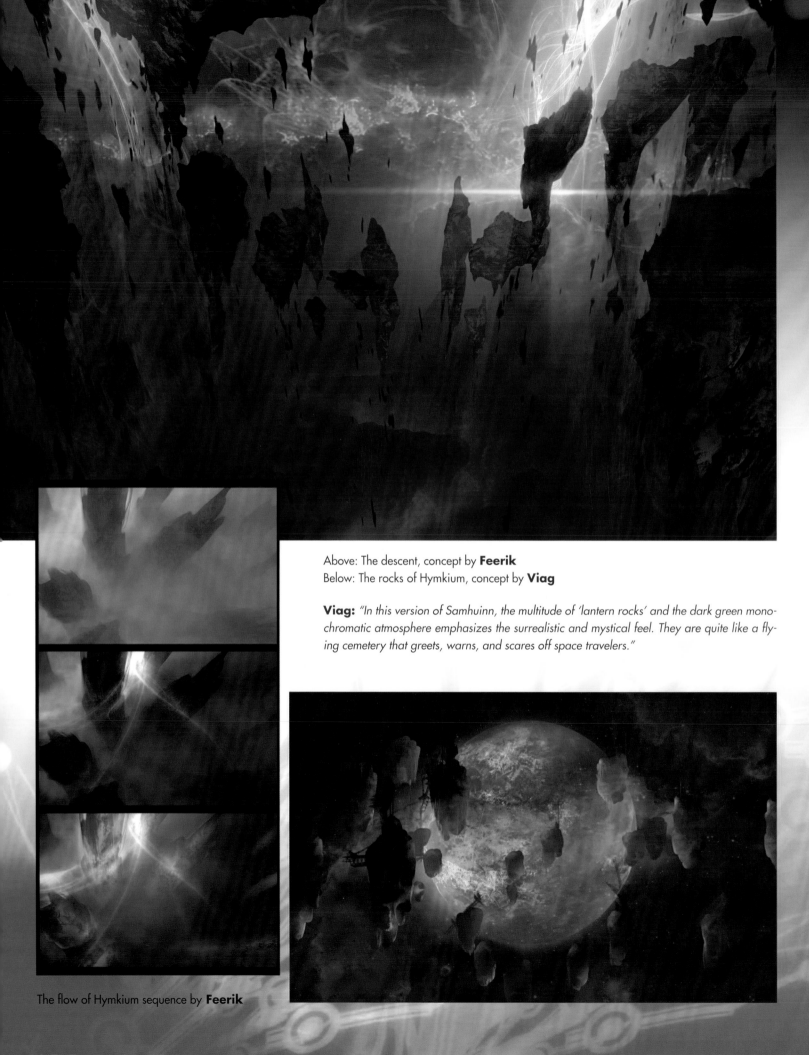

Above: The descent, concept by **Feerik**
Below: The rocks of Hymkium, concept by **Viag**

Viag: *"In this version of Samhuinn, the multitude of 'lantern rocks' and the dark green monochromatic atmosphere emphasizes the surrealistic and mystical feel. They are quite like a flying cemetery that greets, warns, and scares off space travelers."*

The flow of Hymkium sequence by **Feerik**

THE PROMISED WORLD

Samhuinn is not indexed within the S.O.L. galactic map. Surrounded by rocks of Hymkium (a mineral creating random magnetic fields), powerful storms, and a graveyard of wrecked spaceships, access is almost impossible. Only a hothead or a loser would risk his life to get there.

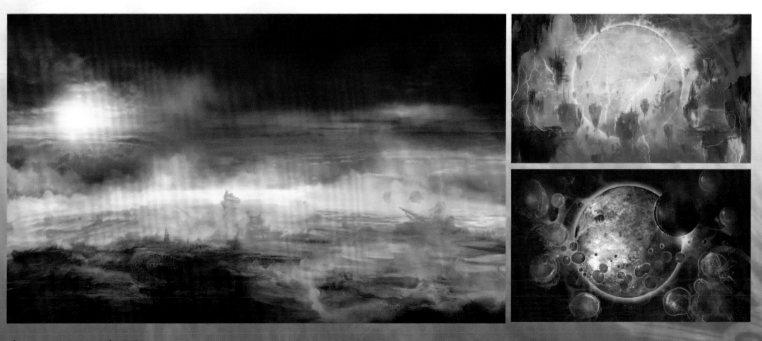

This page: Concepts by **Viag**

Quiet swamps by **Barontieri**

Origin by **Feerik**

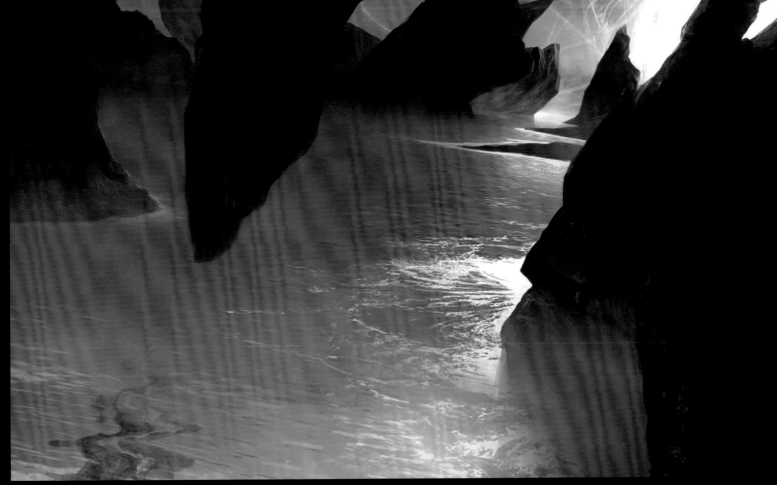

Planitude by **Feerik**

Silent by **Vyle**

141

Viag: *"Once every century the Hymkium rocks that surround Samhuinn lose their magnetic force and land on the planet, crushing the rocks and releasing organic life forms from the rocks' magnetic core. Samhuinnians call this period The Spring of Deaths."*

Barontieri: *"On Jelly Moon, a strange type of jelly-like fluid is holding the rocks together. The crew soon realizes that it bares a resemblance to our Earth oceans, as it hosts a myriad of living creatures."*

Above: Desertic valley by **Viag**

Below: Blobscape by **Barontieri**

Above: Apparitions by **Vyle**
Right: Halloship by **Barontieri**
Below: Apparitions 2 by **Vyle**

Both pages: Concepts by **Feerik**

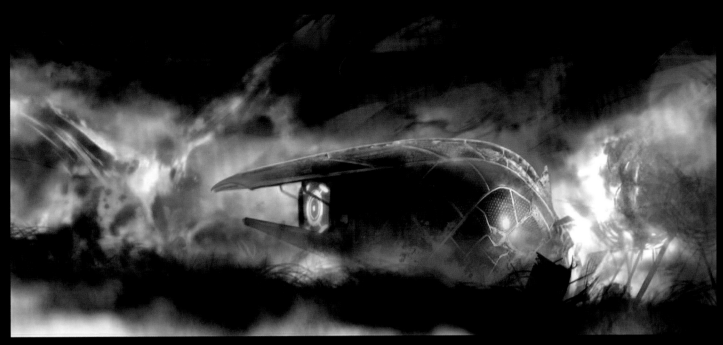

"I survived the black hole. What the hell happened before the crash? I don't remember anything. The module held up better than I thought it would."

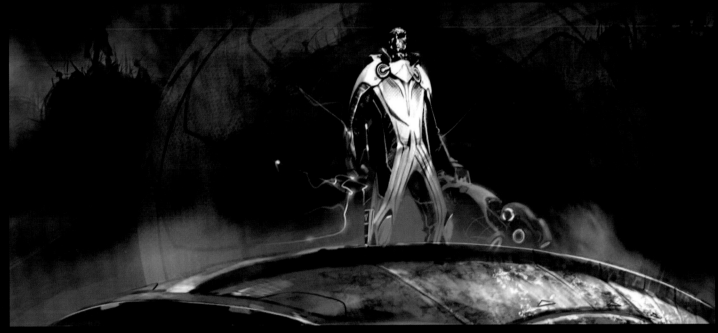

"There it is: Samhuinn. The air is not toxic, just thick. And I'm not alone. They stay silent and motionless, as if I were expected."

"That's the most terrifying thing ever. What is this strange and powerful place?"

147

Concepts by Barontieri and Feerik

HALLOWEENIAN CREATURES

Feerik: *"We started on the concepts for this series with Baron and Viag at the Local 404. We took a full day to draw together what we had discussed the day before. Baron had evoked the idea of insectoid skins that the Samuhinnians could use for protection. Baron and Viag started first while I drew some fast sketches of the dark giants I had in mind, and at the end of the day we merged all the concepts together to create a unique vision. These mini work sessions are essential to us. Unfortunately these moments were so rare, which was quite frustrating!"*

Creature concepts by **Viag, Barontieri,** and **Feerik**

THE DARK GIANTS

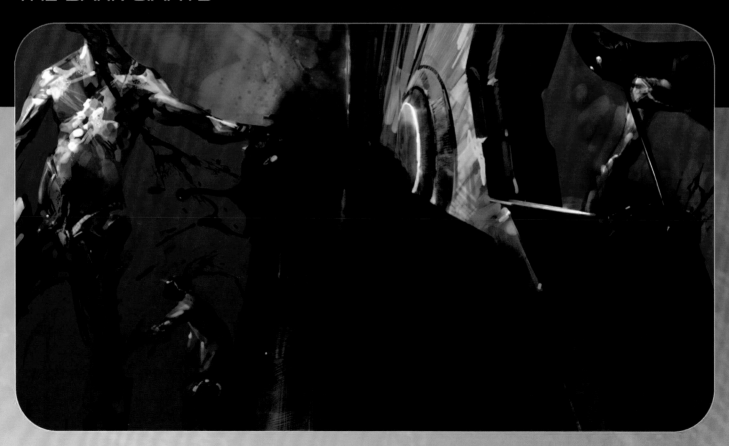

Feerik: *"When I started to design these giants I thought it would be interesting if the black liquid they vomit was to also cause life—birth and death at the same time. The giants are devoted to purification rituals intended to revitalize their fluid, and thus capacity, at the end of their lifetime. These rituals aim to create Ofaha, the precious substance that makes it possible for the children to manifest these same creatures. On Samhuinn, this is the eternal cycle of life, or the life after the death."*

Both pages: Concepts by **Feerik**

Doomed Soul's River by **Vyle**

The attack by **Feerik**

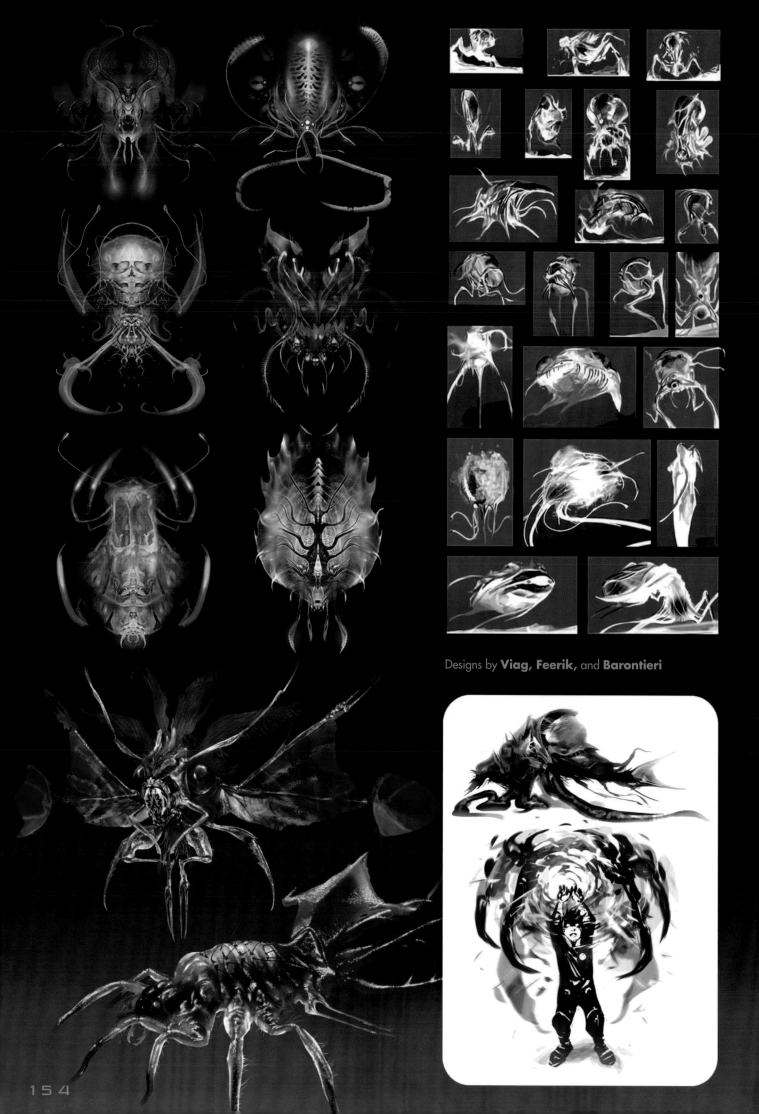

Designs by **Viag, Feerik,** and **Barontieri**

Harry's log: *"Samhuinn is incredible! The variety of species is astounding; I saw gigantic insect-like creatures that are simultaneously terrifying and graceful, ghost-like and colorful. They produce sounds that remind you of Gregorian chants, it's captivating."*

Concept by **Viag**

Concepts by **Viag**

Top left: **Patrick Desgreniers.** Top right: **Rainart.** Bottom left: **Feerik.** Bottom right: **Rainart**

Dark Emperor by Viag

Samhuinnian's eerie army by **Viag**

PASCAL BLANCHE'S BURNED HEAD

SB team: *"To have a guest piece like that in our book is a rare opportunity, and when it comes from an artist and friend as talented and prestigious as **Pascal Blanche,** it's an honor. We've known him now for a few years after working together on several games at Ubisoft Montreal. We learned a lot from him. Pascal is like our big brother, he always keeps a benevolent eye on us and has encouraged us since the beginning of this book project."*

161

Top left: Ofaha bubbles by **Feerik**
Top right: Cache-cache by **Rainart**
Left: Skull Cavern by **Rainart**
Above: CATZ by **Rainart**
Right and middle: Costume
designs by **Barontieri**

les Kidz D'Halloween

Feerik: *"From a young age, the kids are taught to control the Ofaha, the precious substance that allows them to materialize their dreams. This training will cease only at the end of their lives. If a cat has nine lives, a Samhuinnian has many, many more."*

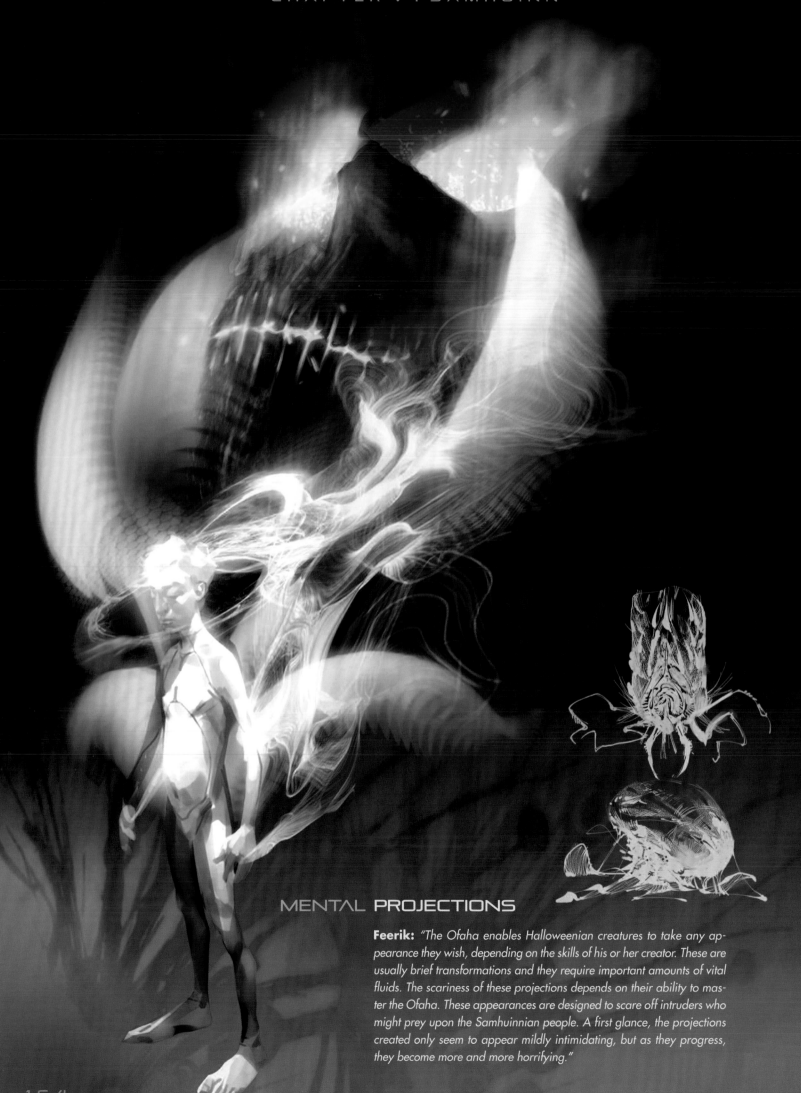

MENTAL PROJECTIONS

Feerik: *"The Ofaha enables Halloweenian creatures to take any appearance they wish, depending on the skills of his or her creator. These are usually brief transformations and they require important amounts of vital fluids. The scariness of these projections depends on their ability to master the Ofaha. These appearances are designed to scare off intruders who might prey upon the Samhuinnian people. A first glance, the projections created only seem to appear mildly intimidating, but as they progress, they become more and more horrifying."*

164

Barontieri: *"I imagined the spaceships as modular, flexible shells, the ship and its pilot form a symbiotic entity which reacts to the environment at a bio-molecular level."*

Top: Sketches by **Feerik,** 1 and 3 by **Vyle,** 2 by **Rainart**

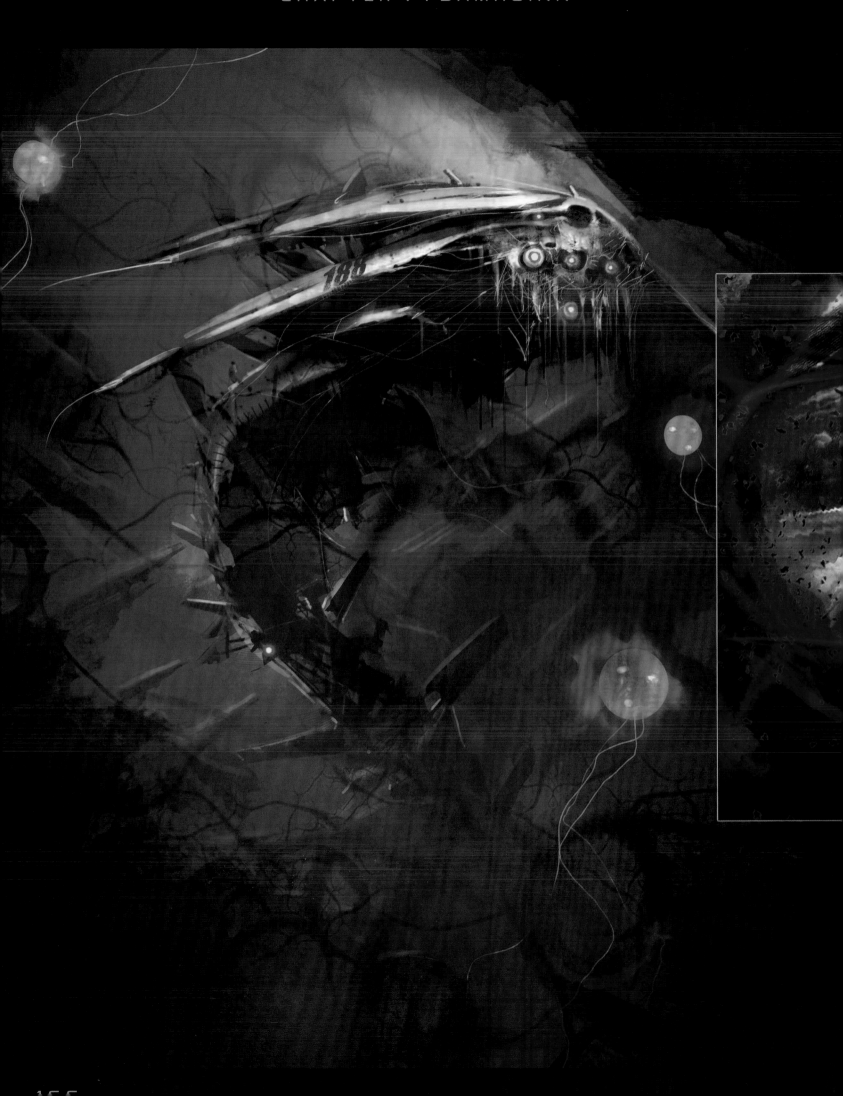

Samhuinnians, humans from the past, colonists, and explorers all recycled their old spaceships and now combine the organic and the anti-material with the strangely dark metals of Samhuinn. Their creepy spaceships are equipped with a soul and are entrenched in the various cracks and crevasses of the planet.

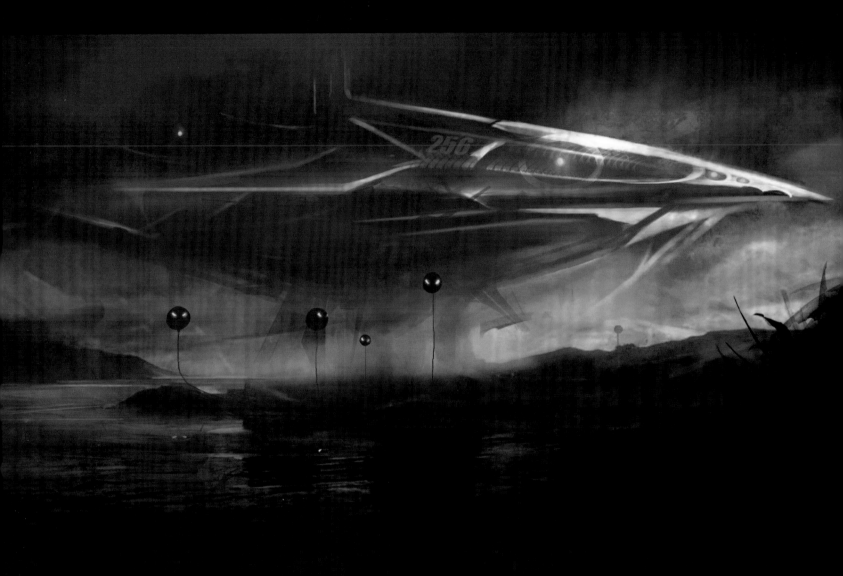

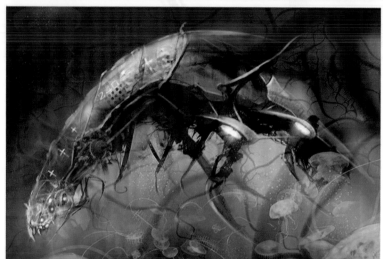

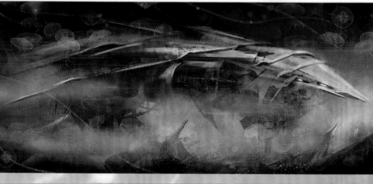

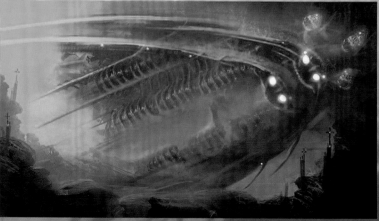

Both pages: Concepts by **Viag**

■ SPECIAL THANKS TO

Scott Robertson and Tinti, all the DSP staff, Travis Bourbeau, David Caplan, the Gnomon Workshop, Dawn Thomas, Brad Booker and Chuck Piel, Reel FX, Bluepoint (kudos to Marco Thrush and Andy O'Neil), Offload Studio, David Giraud, Pascal Blanché, Stephen Duprée, Kynan Pearson, Najd Salas, Nans Bortuzzo, Stéphanie and Cédric Séaut, Marc Goerner, Jean-Eric Hénault, Emile Ghorayeb, Jonathan Abenhaim, Digital 04, ADAPT conference, Paul Hellard, Adrien Annessey, Iain Mc Caig, Dan Milligan, Craig Mullins, ConceptArt.org, Sijun, DeviantART, ImagineFX, Neoformible, CFSL, CG Talk, CG Channel, Eidos Montreal, Ubisoft Montreal, Spacetime Studios, Game Consulting, Julia Delrieu, Elisa Navarro and Masao Kobayashi for their help, Patrick Gagné, Eric Los and Les Barons, Sparth and family, Bruno Gentile, Patrick Lambert, the Ubisoft Campus, Patrice Leymarie, Frédéric Jovet, Nuro, Sébastien Legrain, Jessica Larivé, Marjolaine Roy, Sylvie Bernadou, Caroline Albert, our parents, friends, and families for their eternal support! And of course we are sorry for all those we may forget in this list. We love y'all!

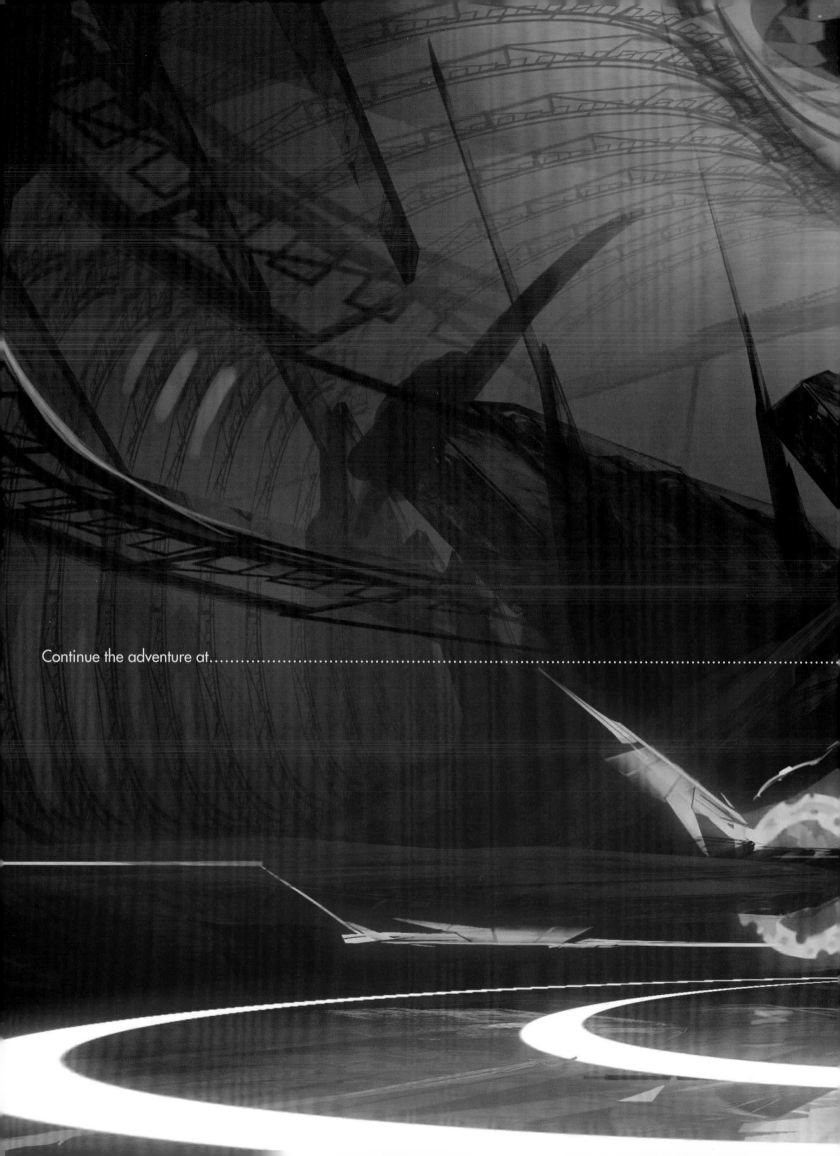

Continue the adventure at..

OTHER TITLES BY DESIGN STUDIO PRESS

ISBN 978-193349251-3

ISBN 978-193349285-8

ISBN 978-193349287-2

ISBN 978-193349227-8

ISBN 978-097266764-7

ISBN 978-193349288-9

ISBN 978-193349249-0

ISBN 978-193349202-5

ISBN 978-193349213-1

ISBN 978-193349215-5

ISBN 978-097266765-4

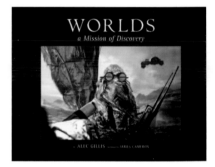

ISBN 978-097266769-2

ISBN 978-193349225-4

ISBN 978-193349201-8

ISBN 978-097266762-3

ISBN 978-193349207-0

ISBN 978-193349204-9

To order additional copies of this book
and to view other books we offer, please visit:
www.designstudiopress.com

For volume purchases and resale inquiries,
please e-mail: **info@designstudiopress.com**

To be notified of special sales discounts throughout
the year please sign up to our mailing list at:
www.designstudiopress.com

Or you can write to:

Design Studio Press
8577 Higuera Street
Culver City, CA 90232

tel 310.836.3116
fax 310.836.1136